RUNNING THE
CORPORATE RAPIDS

JAN '05

CATHI --

THANKS FOR THE OPPORTUNITY
TO WORK TOGETHER.
I CONTINUE TO ENJOY OUR
ASSOCIATION!
BEST OF LUCK FOR CONTINUED
SUCCESS.

RUNNING THE CORPORATE RAPIDS

Creating Agile Organizations

John R. Anderson

To order additional copies of this book, contact:
Xlibris Corporation
1-888-795-4274
www.Xlibris.com
Orders@Xlibris.com
22568

CONTENTS

For Lewis,

without whose friendship, encouragement, wisdom,
and contribution, this book would not have been possible.

FOREWORD

We've tried Quality Circles, we've tried MBO, we've spent millions on TQM programs and, now, we have Reengineered our businesses and still we are not getting the results that we hoped for.

These are the sentiments that an ever-growing number of business leaders are expressing.

Running The Corporate Rapids deals directly with the whys and wherefores of failed management systems and initiatives. It tackles head-on the question of what to do about the current confused situation.

The findings and recommendations in this book are based on author John Anderson's combined 20 years operating experience in business and over 13 years consulting experience working with CEOs and executive teams in a broad spectrum of industries.

Running The Corporate Rapids is a welcome pragmatic, shirt-sleeve guide to transforming traditional corporate cultures into leaner, more collaborative enterprises. It relays *how to actually get the results that you want.* Most of the material is based upon actual, practical experience. You will find here only a minor sprinkling of theoretical premise.

Why have many of these popular systems and initiatives failed to achieve their intended results? The author believes the answer is that we simply have not effectively managed the changes the new systems have brought about in our organizations. Either there has been no management support for implementation or else willingness on the part of individual contributors to support the new model has been missing or those who have been charged with executing the programs lacked comprehension of the consequences. In virtually all cases, there has been a blanket absence of understanding of the impact that the programs would have on people. Moreover, managers and others involved in the initiatives (including consultants) may have lacked the skills to facilitate and manage the change process.

Hal Lancaster, discussing Michael Hammer and James Champy's book *Re-Engineering the Corporation,* notes that " . . . The book, for all its theoretical elegance, glossed over the massive career disruptions caused by the process. Re-engineered work usually requires fewer workers and far fewer managers. Managers resisted, stymieing many re-engineering efforts."* Lancaster quotes author Champy: "I didn't see management to be the obstacle it has been. We've learned how to do the redesign. But the redesign as brilliant as it may be, doesn't get results because of managerial thought and ideology. Either top management isn't aligned behind the change, or others are threatened by a loss of power."

Mr. Anderson observes that often a given system itself would be scapegoated for not achieving specific results and thus discarded in favor of the latest management fad. Over time, employees throughout organizations have built a natural resistance to these highly touted "corporate roll outs," giving rise to a *firmly entrenched cynicism* regarding any new programs that are introduced.

What is wrong with all these initiatives?

Nothing—in and of themselves. The flaw, John Anderson convincingly argues, exists in the application of the systems. We have, as Mr. Anderson perceives, been without a thorough understanding of the impact that these kind of systemic changes have on all the people involved. No understanding, no buy-in. Furthermore, there has been an almost total lack of preparation for the changes by both management and non-management employees.

"Hold on!" managers may say. "We had consultants in to train our people on the new processes and management itself was involved from the very beginning. How dare you claim that we hadn't been properly prepared?"

Specifically—and this is John Anderson's salient point—

---

* Hal Lancaster, "Re-engineering Authors reconsider Re-Engineering," *The Wall Street Journal,* January 17, 1995.

preparation in the form of skill building to grasp the psychological ramifications of major change initiatives in our businesses has for all intents and purposes been ignored. We have taught people about the structures of the new models but failed to recognize any of the psychological implications. Remember: we *train* dogs, but we *develop* people; there is a vast difference.

Running The Corporate Rapids provides readers with a badly needed step-by-step approach to transforming their organization by changing themselves and the people around them. Change is complex, and there are no easy solutions to complex issues. When an organization begins the process of genuinely becoming a world-class, twenty-first century company, there is no turning back. *Things will be different.* We will be operating outside our ordinary comfort zones. We'll be unsure of what to do or how to do it. *Running The Corporate Rapids* is one of the best guides you can own for this kind of journey.

While *Running The Corporate Rapids* is an exquisite road map, it is not the territory. In reality, each situation is different and requires special handling. The era of one-size-fits-all solutions is long past, although frequently we act as if it isn't. Following any one theory or practice in this era of rapid, continuous change is a formula for disaster.

Singular approaches to today's business challenges will absolutely and ultimately not provide the results that we all must have to survive and, indeed, to thrive in our ever-changing environment. Mr. Anderson's message is clear: In today's knowledge-based organizations, *people are our only sustainable competitive advantage.* We *must* invest in them in a way that we have not considered in the past.

John Anderson is challenging us to create *a new common sense for business.* Let us listen carefully to what he has to convey. Much of it may not seem comfortable, but bear in mind Mr. Anderson's operating experience. His ultimate aim is always to strengthen the bottom line.

Forrest E. Miller
Chief Executive Officer
Southwest Bell

INTRODUCTION

Transforming traditional corporate cultures into more agile, responsive organizations is the topic of the day in many organizations.

Early pioneers in this work have missed some of the more crucial elements of organizational transformation and are just beginning to realize that the process involves much more than mere "reengineering." We now know that the amount of time, effort, and skills required by both managers and non-managers for this endeavor are far different from those initially imagined. Transformational work, done correctly, can bring great benefits, but these must be earned through steady practice.

To date, the overwhelming majority of transformational application has been structural in nature, such as Business Process Reengineering, reorganizing, downsizing, and the like. What is too often overlooked in these initiatives is the *psychological impact* that these new structures have on the people who remain.

For more than 100 years in American business, we have literally trained our work force not to think for themselves. *Management does the thinking and employees do the work.* With some of the newer organizational structures (such as cross-functional and self-managed work teams), we have asked employees to take more responsibility for themselves and think about not only what they are doing but also about the impact that their actions have on the business itself.

"Empowerment" has taken on the form of a mandate to "do more with less," which in many cases is an impossibility. The resulting stress has frequently caused an outcome that is the opposite of what was desired.

Organizations that do not have proactive initiatives to help people restructure their thinking will find that simply redistributing the work will not result in a more competitive organization.

If we are to truly transform our businesses into lean, efficient, competitive enterprises, *we are going to have to deal with the attitudes, belief systems, and biases that exist in today's work force.* There is no way around it.

John R. Anderson
San Jose, California

PART ONE

Organizational Transformation: Why Is It Needed?

CHAPTER ONE

How We Got Here

In order to understand much of what we are seeing in business today, it is important to know where we have come from.

In its early phases, American business operated from a paradigm totally different than that of today. Before the Industrial Revolution, workers controlled their entire work process and were thus naturally inclined to improve it because the rewards were immediate. The cobbler made the whole shoe, so he was prone to constructing a better quality shoe for which he could get a higher price. He could make his product more efficiently, enabling him to sell more of it, and he could provide good customer service, thus encouraging repeat business. In such circumstances, there was a direct cause and effect.

A pride in workmanship existed in times past, but this pride has been lost in many segments of our contemporary work force. Most people who were in business way back then operated as sole proprietors or, from time to time, in simple partnerships. This historical closeness to the customer demanded a certain level of quality, service, and value because the customer had direct contact with the supplier and routinely expressed satisfaction and/or dissatisfaction directly to the person performing the work. *There was no place to hide!* Blame was not an option for the producers. If they wanted someone to blame, they might just as well have looked in the mirror. Also, in the past, there existed virtually no mass print media, no electronic broadcast media, and practically no multicity, county, state, or national distribution capability. All of this translated into a need to keep customers satisfied at the local level because, generally speaking, there was no other market to which producers could turn. Local competition competed for local business.

New business was garnered by "word of mouth" recommendation and then, as now, bad news spread at a much faster rate than did good news. Alienate a few loyal customers and you risked losing your entire business.

The old paradigm shifted around the time Henry Ford's ideas about mass production first came into vogue. In order to become more proficient, manufacturing companies brought in teams of industrial engineers and efficiency experts (the clipboard and stopwatch guys) to redesign work processes. Manufacturing jobs were analyzed extensively until the One Best Way for doing a given task was formulated. The thinking was that if management could get the workers to perform a limited number of functions, the workers would then become very skilled at what they did, and assembly lines would run more efficiently. Additionally, given their opinion of the work force in general, management tended to view the individual on the assembly line as just another tool.

People were then "plugged into" these jobs and told just to do the work and not to think about what they were doing because "it's management's job to do the thinking around here." In many cases, the message was even more severe. Either spoken or implied, the message was: "We don't want you thinking about the job and if, in a weak moment, you do happen to think about it, you better never think about changing it or you're fired."

Taking into account the work experience, cultural background, and education of the great majority of the work force at the time, this approach made some sense, as most workers were unaccustomed to operating in such a complex environment. The work force soon adapted to the new rules and became as vested in avoiding responsibility as management was in maintaining the power and control it had achieved. Over the decades, this same logic was applied throughout business in both manufacturing and non-manufacturing jobs. One result is that the worker moved farther and farther away from the customer, fostering an isolationism that resulted in an indifference to consumers. The workers no longer had a direct relationship with customers and therefore felt no loyalty or attachment to them. After all, management called all the shots— it was *their* responsibility to deal with the customers.

Enter blame, which started to play a major role in our business culture. When the worker dealt directly with consumers, they had to take responsibility for customer satisfaction. Now, they could simply blame anything that went wrong on management, the government, or the infamous "them." This business model served us well for many decades, and while it did precious little to develop the work force, it did meet the financial goals of most businesses.

On the surface, this model really did make a kind of sense, as it did meet the most important needs of both the employer and the employee at that time. And while we'll have more to say about such mutual needs in Chapter Two, it is important to note that this structure and the resulting behaviors marked an important milestone in the psychological development of the American worker.

Remember, prior to this new structure, workers had no one to blame anything on and therefore tended to take responsibility for their actions and their customers. Now, they were literally being told to not think about the customer, to not think about the job, and in general, to not think at all. This structure, combined with the condescending attitude of many managers at the time, reinforced the "us" vs. "them" attitude that was beginning to develop.

At many work sites, conditions became utterly intolerable. Physical environments were unclean and unsafe. Work hours and work rules were oppressive, and workers were even physically abused in extreme cases. The resulting polarization and psychological damage is still being felt and acted on in today's work relationships.

One of the methods that the workers employed to combat these intolerable conditions was to form unions, initially in the trades and eventually in all areas of business, including government service. These unions further reinforced the "us" vs. "them" mentality and, ultimately, became as much a part of the problem as the original behaviors exhibited by management. As isolation, level distinction, and class distinction increased, the institutional victimization of the American work force intensified.

Workers' anger at management accelerated. Union leadership did all they could to foster this anger and use it to keep themselves in the positions of power and authority they had created for themselves. In a relatively short period of time, the stage was set for the next 50 or so years. Management had its side, labor its side, and the war was on. Cooperation where it may have existed gave way to deeply held polarized positions around both major and the most minor of issues. Strikes ensued; violence escalated. US vs. THEM, LABOR vs. MANAGEMENT, BLUE COLLAR vs. WHITE COLLAR, COLLEGE EDUCATED vs. NONCOLLEGE EDUCATED, BLACK vs. WHITE, RIGHT vs. WRONG, and on and on.

Enter the government. Beginning with Franklin D. Roosevelt and reaching its acme in "The Great Society," of Lyndon B. Johnson, the government began taking an increasingly active role in the lives of both business and individuals. More government regulations. More social programs. More litigation. Individual rights over the rights of the majority.

Business became the bad guys and the government became the good guys. Individuals had to worry less and less about taking care of themselves. Social Security for retirement; unemployment insurance in case you're out of work; welfare programs if you are unable to work; Medicare and Medicade for health insurance—all at government expense. The underlying message was: "Don't worry, if something bad happens to you, the government will take care of you." These well-intentioned programs were soon translated into entitlement programs, and many believe that the psychological ramifications of the dependency they caused are at the root of a lot of the business and social problems we face today.

Soon, many aspects of these government programs were transferred to business, either in the form of taxes, mandates, or social pressures. The unions jumped on the bandwagon, making "benefits" a major bargaining chip at the negotiating table.

These pressures were seen by much of the private sector as intrusive and unwarranted, so business resisted: "After all, who was going to pay for all of these things?" As business reacted to the rising cost burden of these programs, their resistance to any additional programs hardened. Thus, they were even more at odds with their workers, who by now felt they were entitled to these benefits: "After all, the government says we should have them. If you really cared about us as people you would provide all that we need. We all know that the business owners and managers are keeping all the money for themselves and giving us as little as they can." To various extents, this adversarial model took hold in a great number of businesses.

There is no implication here that management, organized labor, or the government is solely to blame for all of today's ills. The labor/management struggle is simply a vivid example of what has taken place throughout American business. In both union and nonunion environments, the same dynamic is played out day after day. The faceless, nameless "they" are blamed for all the faults of the organization, whether it be at the top management or individual contributor level. "They" are frequently perceived as managers who don't know what they are doing or workers who simply don't care enough to do a good job. Either way, things are not that simple.

In all my experience running businesses, I never once met anybody who actually did not want to do a decent job. Sure, there were those who allowed themselves to be distracted by personal issues, thus affecting their job performance, and those who were so vested in established systems they could no longer make good decisions for fear of retribution from either superiors or peers. I found people who were lazy, not well suited for their job, and unable or unwilling to perform to their optimum level. But I never came across a single person whose first thought in the shower in the morning was, "Let's see, how can I go into work today and really screw things up." People like this almost never find their way to meaningful employment. Either the Social System or the Criminal Justice System ends up dealing with them.

With all of this as a backdrop, businesses have continued to forge ahead with program after program in an attempt to transform their organizations. These attempts have resulted in enormous confusion, turmoil, anger, and fear in the work place. While implementing the new systems, people still "feel" entitled to a certain level of compensation and benefits. They "feel" that they should have job security. They "feel" that they are working as hard as they can and cannot possibly continue to "do more with less."

What we seem to miss in attempting to change our corporate cultures for the better is the impact that these changes have on people *at the emotional level*. Logic has its place in business, but so does emotion, and until we are able to effectively apply both in our day-to-day management practice, we will continue to miss the mark. The leverage that we strive to achieve is available in all organizations but we have not yet figured out how to obtain it. We "know" that we must get more out of our people, and that we must empower the work force. We "know "that we must flatten our organizations. What we have yet to discover is how to accomplish these things while not grinding people up in the process. The "knowing" to which I am referring is the kind that is in our heads. Intellectual knowledge is very powerful and an essential component of any successful business enterprise. There is another kind of knowledge, however, that is equally important: The "knowledge of the heart." Heart knowledge is that instinctive way in which we "know" that we are doing the right thing, with the total absence of any supporting data. It is that special "feel" we have for our businesses, that ability to make decisions about complex issues at a moment's notice. We seem to trust these skills when it comes to the structural/financial aspects of our businesses, but have failed to develop these same skills when it comes to our interpersonal relationships. Achieving a balance between head and heart knowledge in our management practice is where leverage truly lies. Striking that balance begins with examining *our* roles in perpetuating the current realities that we have inherited.

How will we transform our organizations into the productive, competitive entities that they must become? How will we deal with a work force preoccupied with maintaining the status quo? What new skills do employers and employees need in order to prosper in this increasingly competitive global economy? The answers are the keys that will unlock the secrets to success for the world-class organizations of the new century and beyond.

CHAPTER TWO

Times Have Changed

In order to better understand the growth transitions that humans go through, the humanistic psychologist Abraham Maslow (1908-1970) created a model for a Hierarchy of Human Needs. (See p. 25)

Using this famous model, we can see that in the early days of American business, people would work 60 hours a week and more just to meet Maslow's first three levels: food, shelter, and belonging. There was not a great level of consciousness around issues such as balance in one's life, nor was there much thought given to things beyond simple subsistence. In many ways, just getting through each day was challenge enough. The notion of "self-actualization" was first interpreted as a valuable path only by the small psychoanalytical and psychotherapeutic communities. Employers were not aware of the concept, nor were they motivated or even required to provide anything other than money for the work performed by their employees.

Most people felt lucky just to have a job and did not question their lot in life to any great degree. Organized religion, generally speaking, played a greater role in everyday life than it does today, and many people drew comfort from their religion and attributed the difficulties in life to the will of a higher power. This ability to transfer personal responsibility to some higher power helped people survive some very difficult times. As our society began to mature, these simple answers to the complex issues of life became more and more difficult to accept carte blanc. While organized religion still plays an important role in American society, individuals have begun to separate spirituality from it in significant ways. Many people today take a more holistic approach to their lives, so the concept of self-actualization is now fairly common. Balance between work and home life is sought. Quality time with family and friends is a requirement for most workers and managers. Personal growth, both professionally and spiritually, is often a major issue for contemporary workers. In today's affluent society, most people have the first three levels of Maslow's model handled by about Wednesday morning.

This state of affairs raises a question for employers: "What do we offer to our employees for the rest of the week?" Money simply isn't enough when people express a desire for balance in their lives. You frequently hear the phrase "quality of life" in the hallways now where just a couple of decades ago, spending time with family or friends and, in general just *having a life*, wouldn't even have been seriously discussed at work.

There is no doubt: People are looking for different and additional things in their lives these days and most organizations have not yet discovered how to adapt to the new and ever-changing demands of this vocal and sophisticated work force.

On the other side of the ledger, employees are having a tremendously difficult time redefining their own roles in this new business paradigm. While they *want* many of these things in their lives, they believe that it is the employer's responsibility to provide them, and they are frequently unwilling to do the things that *they* need to do in order to obtain them.

In Chapter One, we discussed some of the ways that employees at all levels have been taught to not think for themselves but rather to depend on a fairly small number of people in an organization(management) to do most of their thinking for them.

In order to change these belief systems, *people must be willing to challenge and change some of their most basic beliefs and behaviors.* The entitlement mentality is deeply entrenched in a considerable amount of the work force and letting go of the belief that someone else is responsible for one's welfare, career, compensation, and general well being is a frightening thought for many people. Yet, if we are to succeed in transforming our organizations into flexible, competitive enterprises, that is exactly what must happen.

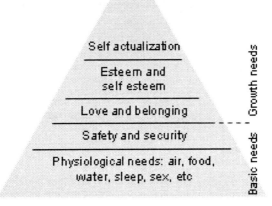

Unfortunately, there exists no clear road map for this transformation. No program, no single process, no seminar or consultant is able to bring a complete, coherent solution to organizational and human transformation situations.

We are addicted to quick fixes. TQM is the answer, Business Process Re-engineering will solve the problems, Self-Managed Work Teams are the Holy Grail, and on and on. We must see almost immediate results or we become frustrated and abandon our efforts in favor of the next hot idea to come down the pike. More training, another reorganization, another consultant and yet one more, so-called, Corporate Roll Out of some program. (If I could exterminate certain phrases from the corporate vocabulary, "Corporate Roll Out" would be at or near the top of the list. I have discovered in my client work that people have seen so many initiatives announced in this manner that when one more comes their way they know that what is to follow is nothing more than another "quick fix" attempt at addressing well-entrenched, complex issues, whether or not this is actually the case.)

People have gotten used to the "fix of the day" approaches and have become desensitized to them. Their eyes glaze over and they go through some internal version of, "I really don't have to change anything about the way that I work. After all, this will only last a few months and it'll be gone. Management is never truly committed to these things, so I don't really have to do anything different." In this behavior, employees at all levels are like children. They will outlast Mom and Dad. They grind away until parents give in and allow them to have their own way.

Men and women have learned to survive in some of the most difficult and frightening modern business environments, and have developed many layers of survival skills. Some of these skills serve well whereas others become as much a part of the problem as the situations that prompted their development in the first place. This book specifically addresses the crucial issue for survivors—developing appropriate skills for managing in the new environment.

In a recent client meeting where we were discussing the prospect of instituting an organizational transformation process, a senior executive asked me if I could present a detailed work plan for the next two years. When my response was "no," he didn't know what to do or where to go next. I explained to him that while there were certain predictable steps that we would take, the response from the people to these interventions were always different, and therefore the results that we would get were largely unpredictable. I further explained that *we* would learn from each step that we took and that our approach would be modified based upon what we learned during the journey. This probably sounded pretty flaky coming from a consultant, and while I understood his concerns, it was the only truthful answer I could give him. I am not by any means implying that transformation work is all at the feeling level (warm and fuzzy stuff) but I am maintaining that it is not always linear, and seldom goes exactly as initially expected. It is, however, the work that the organizations of the future must embrace as a *normal business process, day in and day out,* if they are to continue to grow and flourish.

Indeed, I am engaged in transforming the businesses of my clients daily, actually working on the behavioral and corporate cultural issues involved. Approaches like this are fast becoming an intregal part of corporate America today. What remains unclear is how much lasting benefit we are deriving from the work done to date. What is certain is that our previous attempts to "fix" our businesses by dealing with the structural side while ignoring the people side has not given us the results that we so desperately need.

As the meeting progressed, my client began to understand that this work of organizational and human transformation is not an exact science, and that to get started requires a *leap of faith* of some magnitude.

The truth seems to be that all of the various transformational approaches have some value but that none of them, in isolation, have much impact. As always, we are looking to the outside for our answers, even when we *know* that they lie inside. Remember the telling words of the comic strip character Pogo: "We have met the enemy and it is us."

In Part Two, we provide a specific road map or sequence of events for managers and executives to follow to begin the transformational journey. These steps begin to build the linkage of each individual to their employer in a fashion that is much more personal than the traditional employer/employee relationship.

I emphasized the "we" portion of this response because I believe that it is important for clients to understand that this work is for *them* to do, not a consultant. Consultant-led initiatives in this area of work are one-way roads to disaster. An appropriate role for the consultant in this work is that of the architect, not the builder. Organizational and human transformations must be led by the members of the company, starting with the person at the top.

Company after company tries to change the structure with various programs only to see marginal results, if any. In almost every case, this effort is akin to rearranging the deck chairs on the Titanic. You can force people into new structures and get them to modify their behaviors to a certain extent, but you almost never get true buy-in with this approach. Without the people's buy-in, you can expect marginal change and therefore marginal results at best. In many situations, you get results that are more unfavorable than what you had before you made the changes.

In another client engagement of mine, a new CEO was brought in to change a traditional, hierarchical structure into a flatter, team-based organization. One of his initial moves was to go to casual dress for all employees. Another symbolic move was to remove the doors from all the executive offices at headquarters. Both were reasonable, visible changes to institute, but as with most changes, these were not well understood and, therefore, not well managed. In the old culture, managers competed with "power ties" and two thousand-dollar suits. The CEO's move was obviously intended to relax the atmosphere and create a more open environment.

On a visit to their headquarters location some five to six months after the changes were initiated, I found an interesting behavior among the top managers. They no longer competed using power ties and two thousand-dollar suits—they now competed with expensive sweaters. In fact, it was so obvious to them that *they* referred to the practice as "sweater wars." This was, I thought, a classic example of changing the structure without addressing the belief systems of the people involved. The culture was not about formal attire, it was about internal competition. Any structural change must be accompanied by a testing of the belief systems around the existing structure and how the changes will affect the people involved. Without investing the time and energy to deal with the people issues, organizations will continue to garner minimal results from major, expensive change initiatives.

To repeat: *Individual buy-in is the key to any successful transformation process.* This fact alone mandates that we change the rules about how we treat, recognize, and reward people in our organizations. The one-size-fits-all management approach is no longer effective.

In order to truly engage people at the emotional level (where the decision to really buy-in or not is made), we must find out what each individual genuinely wants and in some way meet all or part of his or her requirements. If this sounds terribly complex, it is.

We are accustomed to having processes and systems that are constructed to serve the organization and make it easy for them to manage the people. In the traditional command and control environment, the needs of the people are of secondary importance and the needs of the organization are paramount. What we are beginning to comprehend is that the people *are* the organization to an extent that they never have been before.

In traditional, resource-based organizations, regardless of what we may have said, the assets that were really valued were the ones that were reflected on the Balance Sheet and the people were merely a means to achieve the financial goals of the company. Over the years, we have certainly given a lot of lip service in our mission and vision statements to people being our most important assets but our behavior seldom reflected the words, especially when things got tight. What is the first thing to get cut from the budget when we're not making plan? Training and education.

We will cut budgets for short-term financial benefit and mortgage our future by missing the one element that could prevent things from getting tight in the first place: *investment in the people.*

In a twenty-first century company, the processes and systems must meet the developmental and emotional needs of its employees in order to keep them engaged. In true knowledge-based organizations, there is a deeply held belief that *people are the only sustainable competitive advantage* and that on-going investment in the human resource is the way to prosper in business. When you think about this belief, the facts tend to support it. In traditional, resource-based organizations, competitive advantage was garnered by having better "stuff" than the other guy—newer technology, more efficient plant and equipment, better distribution systems, and the like. We seem to get precious little advantage out of any of these things anymore, largely due to the rapid rate of change in the world.

Some stark contrasts exist between resource-based and knowledge-based organizations. These contrasts mandate different behaviors if we are to be successful in the new model. For example, in a traditional organization, direction-setting for the business is the sole responsibility of management—primarily, top management. The corporate vision is set at the top. In knowledge-based organizations, "shared visions" emerge from everywhere in the enterprise and are frequently the genesis for new product or service offerings. Top management's responsibility in this environment is to insure that vision exists.

Another contrast is in the area of thinking. As we have noted, most organizations have a culture that requires management to do the majority of the thinking while the workers must simply follow the rules. In knowledge-based organizations, thinking and acting are merged at all levels. Everyone is responsible for using all of their skills and for constantly improving those skills and learning new ones.

Conflict resolution also is handled differently in knowledge-based organizations. Instead of the traditional mediation by management, a continuing dialog and integration of diverse views takes over as the normal process for handling conflict. In this model, everyone bears responsibility for generating the best ideas and solutions. Conflicts are resolved based upon what the best solutions are for the business and the people involved, not for whom is in charge.

It is imperative today that we link employee wants and needs to the mission of the organization. Personal vision and corporate vision must be merged in a way that binds employees emotionally. We can start by paying attention to that most listened to radio station in the world: WIIFM—"What's In It For Me." We all listen to this station every day of our lives. Now it is time to openly discuss our wants and needs in the work place. In Chapter Five, we offer specific methods for creating personal visions and linking them to the mission/vision of the company. Other specific steps are also detailed as part of an overall process of organizational transformation.

By way of example, when I was in the High Tech business, we could get at least five years out of a piece of core technology—FIVE YEARS!! We didn't have to concern ourselves with people issues. The world was beating a path to our door. All we had to do to continue to be successful was to drop a new product on the market that had a few new features every year or so and milk the margin. Our engineering investment was long recovered.

Today, you are lucky if you can get six months. In short,

everybody has got the same "stuff." Bricks and sticks and technology and the like are available to almost everyone and offer virtually no sustainable advantage. So, if you are going to differentiate yourself in the market, if you are to exceed your customer's expectations, you better have the best people with the most flexible systems and the ability to adapt to ever-changing business conditions at a moment's notice. This kind of change does not happen on its own. It takes a concerted effort, over time, and a significant investment of both time and capital.

By all this, I do not mean to imply that the employer has sole responsibility for the success of this new work contract. Quite the contrary! It must be a true partnership, where both employer and employee get what they need.

Each individual in the organization must be clear on what he or she wants and needs and must be willing to share those requirements openly with their team members and team leaders. Additionally, and most importantly, employees at all levels must be willing to take responsibility for their own careers. *They* must bear the burden of building new skills and honing their present ones. *They* must be willing to dedicate themselves to a program of continuous learning and to engage their employer as a support mechanism in this endeavor. *They* must be willing to take on additional responsibility for their own and the organization's success. *They* must develop the capacities to make the tough decisions and stand behind them. *They* must step out of the victim role, abandon the long-standing patterns of apathy and blame, and begin to actually run the businesses.

Our collective job is to learn the new skills required to facilitate these massive changes. Management must be equally willing to challenge and change their beliefs about their own roles and to do the courageous, personal, internal work that will allow them to succeed.

It's time to stop redesigning the past. Let's begin creating the future.

CHAPTER THREE

The Changing Managerial Role

With all that is going on around us, it sometimes seems as if there are no constants any longer and, in lots of ways, that is true. Many of the predictable elements we as managers have always been able to count on in our decision making exist no more. The comfortable, traditional functions of planing, organizing, and controlling in the context of flatter, team-based organizations causes us to rethink how, why, when, where, and even if these functions should be performed in our organizations.

In chapters One and Two, we generally discussed the historic roots of current worksite problems and the changes that have occurred in modern business settings. Now, let's take a more in-depth look, analyzing precisely what has changed and how we can begin to respond to the new paradigms more effectively.

As stated earlier, we in America have inherited a work culture that is based on power, control, and a deeply held belief system that assumes people in most non-managerial roles in organizations are somehow less skilled and less dedicated than those who are in management. While one could argue that such may be true in given cases, I have found both in my own managerial career and in my consulting work that all too frequently the reverse is true. What seems to be a common denominator in my observations is that *different people are skilled in different areas and that what we have done is artificially placed more value on certain jobs.* Thus, divisive attitudes abound: "The white collar worker is better educated and more important than the blue collar worker"; "Management is somehow a higher station than individual contributor roles"; "We're a big deal and you are not."

Now, before you get your hackles up and totally dismiss my point, go a little deeper into the history and culture with me and see if you don't agree, at least to some extent, that what I am saying represents many of your own observations, if not your own experiences.

From the beginning of time there have been the "haves" and the "have nots," a dichotomy that will always hold true to some extent in human societies. There have always been the educated and the uneducated, the cultured and the crass, the powerful and the weak, and the rich and the poor. What we have done in America is created a class system in a country that claims in its very founding documents that "all men are created equal," when we know from experience that this contention is not always so. In my view, the intent of that statement was to convey that all people are entitled to the same opportunities, not that they are, in actual fact, all equal in skill, capabilities, and intellect. The new business paradigm takes this reality into account.

We as managers had set about the task of designing and building systems that guaranteed our ability to retain the power and control we had achieved in the early years and that, indeed, many of us thought was our "right" to hold. Some of our practices were overt (public declarations of our positions and who we were in charge of), whereas others were more subtle (organization charts that showed people "under" managers). Regardless of method, however, the result was the same: We created structured, hierarchical organizations that were controlled by a relatively small number of people (managers) in key positions throughout the organization. We began to carve out our turf within the structure and to build our defenses to guarantee our survival. Power and information was closely held, communication of pertinent business information was limited to a small, select group, and the great majority of the workers were kept in the dark as much as possible.

Status was achieved by moving up the ladder to higher and higher levels in the hierarchy. Every time someone was "promoted," (an interesting word), they moved farther from the workers and the customers. More isolation, less open communication, more resentment. Clubs, formal and informal, were formed. Belonging to the "right" group was paramount to continued success. It's not *what* you know but *who* you know that guaranteed your continual rise in the organization. Individual contribution and performance became less important than how well connected you were politically in the organization. Managers and executives generally were less concerned with mastering their craft than they were with holding on to the power and control. Holding a position in one of the larger organizations reflected one's importance. Empire building became commonplace, and power struggles dominated the managerial landscape. Survival of the fittest in this environment was the norm.

I do not judge these trends as being good or bad. After all, I was a part of the same system for many years. My purpose in emphasizing the history here is strictly to reinforce the picture of how strongly our business cultures have been biased in a certain direction.

With our history being part of our current reality, our organizations have begun to evolve into a different type of system, one based on the changing work force, the economic demands of the times, and a new level of awareness by all members of organizations. What awareness? The one that tells us that what we have been doing for many years is just not working as well as we need it to work today. *Transformation is mandatory.*

Chapter Five suggests some specific steps to take to begin the journey of transforming yourself and your organization. Part of the process involves continuous learning, which is a constant in all that I do and all that I talk and write about. The question is, continuous learning about what? In traditional organizations, mangers would, from time to time, participate in some continuing education, usually around their particular area of technical expertise. The Controller or CFO would study the latest accounting techniques or tax laws and regulations. The R & D manager would attend seminars and workshops on the latest technical innovations. Sales managers would participate with the troops in sales training, and so on. It seems that most of us would only take steps to sharpen our management skills when forced to. Who needed it? We were in charge.

The more progressive organizations today are beginning to appreciate the reality that other than conventional skills are required to manage effectively. Many of these additional new skills are driven by the changing organizational structures that have been implemented in the many and various attempts to streamline, cut costs, and respond to the demands of the marketplace.

Consider, for example, some of the "givens" we have been able to depend upon for many years in our business careers and contrast them to the new situations we find ourselves in today. Some of the stark contrasts are illustrated in the accompanying THEN and NOW chart.

THEN	*NOW*
Lifetime employment	Employability
Steady advancement	Lateral movement
Hierarchy and a career model	Career self-management
Defined benefit pensions	Defined contribution pensions
Office	A laptop and flex time
Supervision and evaluation	Team management
9 to 5 and paternalism	Freedom to challenge

Employability versus Lifetime Employment

When you study the contrasts, some interesting themes begin to emerge. For years, lifetime employment was not even an issue. In the early days of American business, 30 years on the job and a gold watch upon retirement was considered the norm. People would spend their entire career with one employer and retire after several decades of "loyal service." As our businesses and society evolved, however, managers began to move from company to company with increasing frequency. It reached a point in the 1970s and 1980s where it was commonplace to switch jobs every two to three years without the prior stigma of being a "job hopper."

The days of "30 years and a gold watch" are gone forever. The paradigm of "lifetime employment" has given way to an era of "individual employability." What is meant by individual employability? It is having the skills to be employed in a wide variety of circumstances and environments. To remain employable today, people have to develop "transferable skills," skills that can be applied in different companies or in different areas of the same company. During the 1980s, if you were an "expert" in some field, you could just about write your own ticket. People who were an inch wide and a mile deep were sought after for their particular expertise and were well compensated for their talents.

While the market is still in need of so-called experts today, these positions are far less available than they were twenty years ago. Currently, more and more employers are looking for people who have developed a wide range of skills and expertise, and who can adapt to the ever-changing business landscape. For instance: the marketing person who has invested the time in learning about finance and accounting or the engineering manager who has invested in his or her MBA, or the human resources professional who has developed a broad knowledge of several facets of the business.

For years, we hired people based upon their experience in a given field. Having a strong resume was the first step in even being considered for a position. People would say, "I've got 20 years experience in the business." What we are beginning to understand is that *many of these people have one year's experience, twenty times.* There is a world of difference here. Today, people are considered for many positions far less for what they have done in the past and far more for what they may be capable of doing in the future. Now, one's resume is secondary. What's primary, what counts, is *attitude* and *aptitude.* If potential employees have a positive attitude about learning and change and if they display the aptitude for those things, they are a viable candidate.

Lateral Movement versus Steady Advancement

In the era of specialization, steady advancement up the hierarchy was almost guaranteed if you practiced your craft well and kept your nose clean. In fact, for a long time in many of the Bell Operating Companies, managerial positions were generally a two-year assignment. All you had to do to get promoted was to do a reasonable job and not challenge the status quo. Not rocking the boat has become the hallmark of many hierarchical organizations, and is one of the root causes of the problem of people being unwilling to accept responsibility for their work and their actions. These types of structures foster a "caretaker" mentality and are the antithesis of what is required to succeed in business today. (Imagine the cultural struggle that companies with this kind of history are having in trying to become competitive and customer-focused in the modern marketplace.)

Today, lateral movement is where the opportunities lie. In years past, a lateral move within an organization was the death knell for a career. A lateral move then meant that you were passed over for promotion and that your career with that organization was, at best, sidetracked and often, for all intents and purposes, over. Today, we are looking for individuals with a wide variety of experiences and talents. The emphasis is on those possessing "transferable skills." Such people are the most employable and promotable of any in the workforce.

Career Self-Management versus a Career Model

A related but slightly different contrast exists between the old "hierarchy and a career model" and "career self-management." As mentioned, having rungs in the career ladder provided a model for advancement within a given organization and offered ample opportunity for promotion. With all of the downsizing and re-engineering accomplished in the current business environment, many of the rungs of the ladder no longer exist. There just aren't as many places to go "up" in most organizations.

So, where are the opportunities? They are literally everywhere in companies that are beginning to appreciate the power of the newer organizational models and who have learned that doing more with less is often not realistic. What is realistic, is doing the appropriate or vital things with less by applying the total human resource in new and innovative ways.

Career self-management means taking responsibility for building the skills and expertise that will allow you to be successful in a wide variety of situations. Each of us must realize that if we are not improving our ability to contribute to our organization, every day, we are obsoleting ourselves as we sit there. Another way to think of this is: If we are not on a continuing education binge, we are becoming more unemployable as each day passes. Career self-management is an issue for both the employee and the employer. In the new work environment, it is the responsibility of the employee to initiate his or her own self-development, and the responsibility of the employer to "partner" with the employee in this endeavor. Both parties should bear some of the burden for this new work. The employer may choose to provide certain training and development opportunities and the employee may have to devote personal time to take advantage of these opportunities.

Contribution Pensions versus Benefit Pensions

In the realm of security and benefits, many organizations, for years, provided employees with pension plans that were partially or totally funded by them. In a defined pension plan, monies are contributed by the employer to a pension plan each year regardless of the financial performance of the company. For decades, financial performance, shareholder dividends, and the general health and welfare of many organizations were put at risk by this practice. It was another way for corporations to "take care" of its employees or in the broader scope of things, to control the employees by binding them financially to the organization. This practice was obviously a double-edged sword. On one hand, people tended not leave organizations where they were fully vested in these type of programs. On the other, the programs themselves did little or nothing to provide employees with incentives to maintain or improve their productivity. Regardless of how well employees did, or how the company performed financially, employers "owed" workers the contributions.

Today, many companies have transitioned to programs that are tied both to individual productivity and the overall financial performance of the organization. These, "defined contribution programs" represent a much more realistic approach to pension plans. In many of these plans, employees assume responsibility for direction of the funds within the plans and manage the investments themselves. Employers are providing financial planning seminars and other forms of education for their employees, and leaving the ultimate decisions up to them.

The Portable Electronic Office versus the Fixed Office

The old model of having an office in a fixed location is being replaced in many circumstances with the so-called "virtual office." Job functions that are largely "in the field" are now supported with technology (such as laptop computers/PDA's, and cellular telephones) instead of traditional offices and support staff. If it is to succeed, this structural change must be followed with appropriate behavioral changes. People need to develop the skills of computer literacy, time management, self-motivation, and others to work effectively in an environment where they are their own support staff and where there is no direct supervision and/or peer pressure to perform.

As with most things in life, there is both good news and bad news in the virtual office structure. The good news is that we are able to take advantage of technology to its fullest while controlling overhead expenses for offices and support staff. Relatively new technologies (such as video conferencing and the Internet) as well as the more established advances (such as cellular telephones, voice mail, electronic mail, and teleconferencing) have provided us with the ability to communicate voice and data information twenty-four hours a day, seven days a week with almost no delay. On the surface, these technologies seem to be an incredible boon to business. Instantaneous communications of business information on a worldwide basis should provide us with a competitive advantage in the global market but once again, we have largely forgotten about the effects these technological advances have on people.

One of the major components of our mental tool kit that has been compromised by these technologies is our need to contemplate before decision making. Whether the matter involves governmental world affairs or how to price a competitive bid, we now are required to provide immediate answers to many complex issues. This pace of information movement has added new layers of pressure and stress on people, and many continue to struggle with the consequences. Moreover, the virtual office has removed the affiliation or social component from many work situations, causing feelings of isolation and in severe cases, depression. People are tribal by their very nature, and require a certain amount of human contact. When this is largely removed from our work lives (where we spend the majority of our waking hours), the effects can be devastating.

Organizations and individuals operating in this manner or considering moving in this direction should be diligent about providing structured situations where workers are provided with face-to-face interactions with their colleagues. For example, many geographically dispersed sales organizations teleconference every other week to track their progress towards sales goals and provide some group interaction. They intentionally meet personally once per quarter for face-to-face interaction. Also, headquarters personnel and people from other regions must make the time, when traveling, to personally visit the virtual workers in the area they are visiting.

Team Management versus Supervision Management

Conventional supervision and evaluation is being replaced with the concept of team management, which is largely self-management. Instead of management by inspection, we are giving way to a system of management by expectation. Instead of supervisors and managers looking over the shoulders of their direct reports, they must manage by negotiating mutually agreeable goals and expectations and holding people accountable for specific results.

This new model requires vastly different skills from managers, who must learn to adjust internally. Inspection must be replaced with coaching. Top-down direction and goal setting is replaced with a more collaborative negotiated model, and personal accountability replaces blame.

Working Freedom versus Paternalism

The 9 to 5, paternalistic environment where employees were expected to follow all the rules is being replaced by a flexible, geographically dispersed work force that has the right and is, indeed, expected to challenge the status quo as part of their normal job. This new environment has stirred up a lot of controversy, and has caused both management and non-management employees to question their ability and even their willingness to make the changes required to function under the new rules. Operating in these new environments require skills that many managers have not fully developed, if even gained.

In the traditional work environment (where you could manage by getting up from your desk and looking around), management by control and inspection was possible and was the method most everyone employed. Disagreements from subordinates were treated as problems rather than valuable information, and compliance with the rules was expected. In the new work environment, however, in order to survive, managers and employees alike must develop the skills of positive confrontation, systemic problem solving, continuous improvement, and change management.

With all of the discussion of change and new skills, managers and executives alike have frequently viewed this evolving business culture with dread. In my client work, I have had senior executives say to me, "You mean I have to give up everything I've learned in the past 25 years?" To questions like these, my answer is always a resounding "NO!" This is not a process of giving up, but rather of adding to. Many of the skills we have acquired over the years are valuable, and it would be inappropriate for us to think that we cannot use them. What we are talking about is developing a more robust managerial tool kit for each of us to use.

If the only tool you have is a hammer, you treat everything like a nail. There are times when being directive just makes good sense and there are times when being more facilitative is a better approach. The key is to know which tool to use in given situations. For instance, if the building is on fire, we're not going to sit around gaining consensus on what to do. Someone is going to pull the directive tool from their bag, bark some orders, and get people moving. On the other side of the coin, we may get more value from our planning process by involving a broad range of people in a series of meetings over a period of several months. This approach is a good investment of time, and managers need to become more skilled in facilitating the process rather than deciding on the specific content of the plan itself.

A Case In Point

In a recent client meeting, I observed an inspiring example of a CEO knowing what tool to use when. This was a professional engineering firm with a history of growing by acquisition. Over the past few years, productivity had declined and they were experiencing many of the classic post-acquisition problems. People were hanging on to their old identities, units were operating in various stages of isolation, services were being duplicated by individual units, and business opportunities were not being referred internally, to name just a few. After losing several million dollars the year before, a new CEO was brought in to "turn things around." During his first year he really picked the place up and shook it. Corporate staff was reduced from 28 to 6. Autonomous units were merged and consolidated, people were terminated or reassigned, overtime was eliminated, and base wage levels were frozen. In addition, a true "pay-for-performance" system was installed and the good-old-boy network within the company was crushed. You can well imagine the shock and resulting turmoil that all these sweeping changes caused. Virtually all the steps were taken without the involvement of the other employees, except for human resources and legal counsel.

With their first year under the new leadership coming to a close, the CEO invited me in to talk about how to make the changes stick and how to build a strong consensus around the new vision and structure he had created. He had done all he could to structure the company around his vision of a seamless organization that offered high-quality products and services in a challenging and rewarding, pay-for-performance environment. To his great credit, he realized that in order to have lasting change, the firm needed to invest in helping the people who remained (the survivors) adapt and embrace the new rules. He was also aware of his lack of knowledge and skill in this area, and was prepared to surround himself with a support system that could coach him and offer services directly to the employees.

In short, this CEO did what was necessary to stop the bleeding and position the company for success in the future. He was also critically aware that, in order to achieve the stated vision, they were going to have to do a lot of work on the culture and that he and his team were going to have to develop additional skills in order to succeed.

The New Skills

We have used the phrase "new skills required" throughout and have warned that they are absolutely necessary for your survival. What, exactly, are these skills?

Generally speaking, managers know how to operate in the command and control environment: Providing direction, setting goals, designing control and feedback systems, and monitoring people while maintaining some "subject matter expertise" in their chosen field are all skills that have served managers well. The traditional managerial functions are still needed in any well-run enterprise. What must be different today is who is doing them and how they are being done.

In an atmosphere of individual responsibility and empowerment, managers *must be willing and able to let go of much of the traditional power and control.* We must begin to place emphasis on our functions as developers of people rather than on our roles as orthodox directors of business.

In his book *The Fifth Discipline*, (Doubleday/Currency, 1990), Peter Senge defines the new management mission as building learning organizations. He describes the five disciplines required: Systems Thinking, Personal Mastery, Mental Models, Building Shared Vision, and Team Learning. The development of these skills throughout organizations is imperative if one is to shape an organization that truly learns and teaches as part of routine business process.

Systems thinking deals with issues of seeing the interrelationships of all people and systems within an organization. To practice and learn this discipline, we must redirect our energies to dealing with root-cause issues rather than treating symptomatic signs. We must learn to "see" systems, not snapshots; focus on patterns, not single events; and learn how our businesses and the people in them really operate. Thinking in this way enables us to move *beyond blame*, and to begin addressing business issues as such rather than as personal issues. Systems thinking will require us to change our perceptions of ourselves, our co-workers, and our businesses.

The difficulty in developing these new skills is that they challenge many long-held beliefs. Just saying you must learn them is not enough, you must dedicate yourself to actively working on them. Many of the tools presented in Chapters Five, Six and Seven can help you to discover things about yourself that will enable you to embrace this new way of thinking and managing. It requires hard work and sometimes it feels as if you are going two steps forward and three back but as I have mentioned, you must be in this for the long haul. Introspection and self-discovery can be a difficult process, so be gentle with yourself. Go slowly and seek advice and counsel from family, friends, and professional practitioners. Our addiction to crisis management and quick fixes is strong. It will take hard work and time to begin to see the interconnectedness of systems and behaviors in your business. Creating the culture to support this new thinking style is paramount to fostering new growth.

Personal mastery involves developing your capacity to clarify what is most important to you. The Personal Vision Statement (see p. 97) and its linkage to your employment situation discussed in Chapters Five and Six is but the first step in the development of personal mastery. You must next define the skills required to succeed in your chosen field and put in place an action plan for developing and honing those skills as part of your everyday work life. When we articulate what we really want to be, we create commitment to it. *Compliance comes from serving someone else's vision; commitment comes from living one's own.* The practice of personal mastery includes clarifying what we really want and telling the truth about current reality.

Mental models have to do with how we perceive our world and our role in it. In a continuous learning culture, we must remember that learning is natural and motivation is intrinsic. My model for normal is a three-year-old child. Think about kids. They can't wait to get to each day to discover what's new, what's to be learned, and what's to be experienced. They have a zest for learning that springs from a natural motivation. "Why?" is the one question that small children ask you over and over, driving you crazy. Kids are born with an innate curiosity and passion for learning new things, tinkering with old things, and generally creating their own new world each day. Through our systems of parenting, education, and business, we manage that natural motivation right out of our kids so by the time they get into their middle twenties, most of them have learned to suppress their natural passion for learning, creating a nation of rule followers. Managers must learn to find that original zest for learning new things within themselves, nurture it, and transfer that passion to others in the organization.

A key to forming mental models can be found in the art of inquiry. Most of our training in communications and conflict or problem resolution is based upon the adversarial model. We have learned how to argue and to advocate for a particular position, but relatively few of us have learned how to inquire into a different point of view without creating polarization. Inquiry allows examining apparent disparate views without invoking the typical responses we are all familiar with when a particular belief or opinion is challenged.

Inquiry requires our letting go of certain assumptions that we may hold about the subject matter at hand or the people involved in the dialogue. Over a number of years as a management consultant, I have developed a technique that has allowed me to use inquiry quite effectively. I was having a difficult time giving up certain assumptions concerning various issues and when doing so experienced a feeling of loss, which caused me to severely resist "letting go." To deal with this feeling, I determined that I did not have to "give up" anything, but rather could hold my beliefs and assumptions in a way that allowed me to truly listen to a different point of view and inquire into it without negative psychological effects.

The mental model I use for this practice is that of the hologram. I literally practice suspending my assumptions in midair and view them as a three-dimensional color picture of my beliefs. Having this picture readily available to me (within arm's length, so to speak) allows me to access my beliefs at any time while comparing an opposing point of view in a rational, logical manner. Nothing has to be given up. I don't even have to change my mind about the particular subject. What I do have to do is consider the opposing point of view analytically. My thoughts now are, "Isn't this interesting? This bright, capable individual holds an entirely different point of view about this subject that I do. Why is that? Is there something here for me to learn?" Practicing this technique gives me the skill to ask better questions, to bring out sensitive issues in a non-threatening way, and to generally learn more about the systemic (as opposed to symptomatic) business problems that my clients face.

Now, I don't make a big deal about going through this process. It is done silently, in the privacy of my mind, and is but one of many new skills I believe modern managers need to develop in order to be more effective. To surface mental models that individuals hold, we must become skilled at asking questions in a constructive, non-threatening way. After all, these mental models are what drive individual behaviors. More often than not, we behave according to what we believe rather that what we know.

Building shared vision can be accomplished organizationally in any number of ways, so I don't claim to have the only effective version. I do, however, have the benefit of having experienced all sides of the issue over the years. As an employee, an employer, and a consultant, I've participated in and observed this process many times, and have come full circle in my thinking about it.

In hierarchical organizations, vision comes from the top and is disseminated downward with the implicit message that all should get behind it and support it. It *is* what the boss wants to see. In flatter, more team-based organizations, visioning is a collaborative process with many groups and individuals involved. Both methods have certain value. The traditional version fosters compliance whereas the team-based version often fosters commitment. The question then becomes, "Compliance or commitment to what?" To build a world-class organization, I believe we must have both compliance to certain core values and commitment from all the people involved to support the direction of the company, within reason.

Unless human beings evolve to a point where things such as competitiveness, self-serving behavior, blame, and jealously are no longer part of who we are, we will always need a certain amount of direction to work together towards a common goal. In an ideal environment, everyone would be skilled in Senge's five disciplines (and more) and would always behave according to those guiding principles. The reality is that some adhere to the principles, some do not, and many do so on a part-time, on again, off again basis. Our job as managers is to partner with those who do, help those who are willing to learn, and weed out those who cannot or will not.

Experience has taught me that the person who sets the cultural tone of the organization (usually the CEO) is most effective when he or she is clear about core values, communicates those values regularly, and sets, along with the board, the general direction for the company. Simply put, it is incumbent upon the leader of the organization to define the conditions of employment at the highest level. Leaders must articulate two things: "Here's how you get hired around here; here's how you get fired around here. Now, in between those two events, you have a great deal of latitude in how you execute the work here, but there are certain conditions of employment." Setting the cultural tone for the organization is the responsibility of the CEO or whomever is held accountable for the overall success of the enterprise.

This foundation-laying provides everyone an opportunity to test their own values against those of the organization and to decide, based on real data, whether or not they are in the right place. Once that decision is made, the processes discussed in Chapters Five and Six begin the task of building shared vision in the organization. Shared vision is not always in direct compliance with the overall vision of the company. We should allow enough flexibility for a variety of visions to emerge from every level of the organization as long as they are not in conflict with the core values. These apparently disparate visions are often the genesis of new product or service initiatives, new organizational structures, or other vital components that are key to overall success.

Team learning assumes that organizations and teams, like individuals, have the capacity to learn. Along with that capacity comes certain learning disabilities as well. While individual learning is vital to the success of any enterprise, team learning is equally important and, in many ways, more beneficial. Team learning takes practice and requires application of the four other disciplines to be effective. We must become more intentional in our chartering of work teams to include team learning as a component of the group's mission. A committed group that is intentionally increasing its capacity to learn and achieve is where true leverage is created. Groups that function with these disciplines are energized, creative, and magical in their thinking. They *are* the difference between ordinary and world-class organizations.

All of the roadblocks to team learning reside in our belief systems and the behavior resulting therefrom. We discuss some of these barriers, such as confusing what you do with who you are. Whenever there is a great emotional attachment to one's particular job function or title, it is frequently difficult if not impossible for team learning to occur. At some psychological level, you are always protecting your position, and will consciously or unconsciously ward off any attempts to change your situation.

Blame is another major learning disability for teams. When blame becomes an accepted part of the culture, it is all too easy to transfer the responsibility for substandard performance or failure to someone else or some other group. This ability to deflect responsibility for things gone wrong is one of the biggest problems we face in our society and, consequently, in our business enterprises. There can be no place for blame in a healthy organization. Blame is the great emotional escape. It is a free ride at the expense of our colleagues and the overall organization. We must do all we can to build a corporate culture where we remain focused on resolving the root cause issues that result in our problems and not get distracted by the easy way out----placing blame.

One of the most common learning disabilities in organizations involves our fixating on short-term events. By focusing on symptoms rather than the underlying causes, we continually repeat the same mistakes. How many times have you heard yourself say, "Why are we always solving the same problems?" The reason is that our problem solving is usually only applied at the surface level. Time is not invested in determining core issues and repairing the source of the problems at their root, which brings substantive, not temporary, advantage.

Another learning disability is what Senge calls "The Myth of the Management Team." In the great majority of my consulting relationships, I discover groups of people throughout organizations that refer to themselves as teams, but really function as something quite different. Most so-called teams are actually a collection of bright, capable people who meet together as a group, from time to time, to deal with specific business issues. The most common example of this ad hoc getting together is our top management or executive teams. A true team shares a common vision and works together, intentionally, to achieve it. The vision most often is an integration of personal vision with the work team mission and in exceptional organizations, it includes continuous learning as one of its prime values.

There are certain things that help to promote individual and team learning, such as a belief that differing opinions or assumptions are opportunities to explore. Different or even opposite points of view can be integrated into a stronger understanding of the issues. Mistakes are opportunities for learning, not for blame. If we can learn to treat errors and failures as normal parts of the business process, we can take them as opportunities for learning. What we typically do, however, is look for someone to scapegoat in order to absolve ourselves of any responsibility. Fear and blame will stifle learning faster than anything I am aware of.

Another opportunity for team learning is based in adopting a belief that we can change anything, once we decide we want to. If we choose to be nobody's victim, we can operate in a truly empowered manner, and will not be constrained by the past.

Lastly, we have to be ready for the apparent chaos that results from letting go of many of our long-cherished beliefs and behaviors. There is a natural fear that accompanies any major change and we must learn to trust our instincts and to believe that we are pursuing the right course. We must always bear in mind that the future of American business lies in Learning Organizations.

Applying the New Skill

In redefining the managerial job, we have talked a lot about learning and some of the new skills required. Now, let's look at a number of specific areas where we can learn and apply these new skills.

When we think about management, most of us get a picture of someone who is in charge. While that may not necessarily change, what will change is what is meant by being in charge. Managers have traditionally been responsible for making most of the decisions, doing the majority of the planning, and making sure things get done. In flatter, team-based organizations, those things still need to be done; however, individual team members are doing most of them. So what are managers to do?

Traditionally, we were charged with building and protecting the assets of the corporation. We were measured by how well we built a strong balance sheet, how much we grew the business, and how much return on investment we delivered to the shareholders. If you think I am going to say that we will no longer be held accountable for these things, don't. The reality, in business, is that we will still have to deliver these things. In many ways, it is still our job. What we are talking about here is a more efficient, effective way to deliver them.

One of the first internal changes we must accept is that our role as managers is changing, and will continue to change. Instead of "being in charge," we must begin to think of ourselves as more of a support to those who are really running the business—our employees. Instead of our traditional images as planners, organizers, and controllers, we should begin imagining ourselves as designers. Increasingly, the managerial job is that of designers of systems and work processes. Your work must become more strategic in nature and less hands on at the technical level. Remember, most of your training and experience is in whatever particular area of expertise you developed as individual contributors. It is your comfort zone, and for decades you have been expected to possess, and have been rewarded for, your knowledge in these areas. Even when you moved into management, you were expected to remain the chief authority on the subject matter of the area you managed.

When I said to think of yourself as a designer of systems and processes, what I mean is that your job must become one of looking at the organization from a higher level and beginning to see the interconnectedness of all of its components in a different way. This is a primary area where systems thinking applies. More of your energy must go into the design of the organization and the development of its people. In resource-based organizations, your command of the technical aspects of your area of responsibility was paramount, but in knowledge-based organizations, your ability to design, educate, and adapt are your most valuable assets.

Begin to see your organization as the living system it is. Look for areas of health and areas for improvement. Find out why some parts of the business function better that others. Learn what those areas do well and get the people in it to transfer that learning to other departments. Put your efforts into initiatives that will improve the ability of your company to deliver quality products and services to your customers. Seek ways to improve customer service and responsiveness.

Remember, your work within organizations dedicated to continuous learning and customer delight now becomes discovering what people know and believe, and engaging them at a different level. All the customer service training, total quality management initiatives, and other "programs" you have experienced will fail to provide the results you want until you become skilled in understanding *why* people do what they do in addition to *what* they should be doing.

As a designer of organizations and processes, you become the engineer and the architect. Individual contributors in your organization become the contractors. In other words, you design the building, and they build it. Using construction as a metaphor for management may seem like a bit of a stretch but if you have ever been involved in construction, you know that edifices are seldom built according to the original specification and drawings. Contractors make changes to the design all the time. Individual workers change, modify, and add to the design on a daily basis in order to achieve the end results—a quality structure, on time and on budget. Now I know that everyone has a horror story about construction, but that is not the point. What is important in this analogy is that models exist where those who are "in charge" are not involved in the specific work tasks and leave much of the responsibility for implementation to the people doing the work.

Next, begin to consider yourself as a teacher. More and more, CEOs are being referred to as Chief Education Officers. In flatter, knowledge-based organizations, there simply are not as many people to produce the work. Gone are the hoards of staffers, supervisors, and managers who used to perform many of the administrative functions. Some of these functions may no longer be required; some may fall into the category of "nice to do" but are not "vital to do" and, therefore, can no longer be afforded; still others need to be done, and this work must be redistributed among those who remain. Developing the new skills around human behavior will allow you to coach effectively, help people move beyond blame and fear and become open and even enthusiastic about learning the new things they must know to succeed.

As a teacher, inspire others in your company by setting the example for learning new things. Don't muffle your excitement about the prospects for the future. Have some fun with this. If you view these new duties as drudgery, so will the others in your group and throughout the company. If you provide a learning environment and the rewards and recognition systems that support this new behavior, you are much more likely to be successful in transforming your organization.

Think of yourself as a steward of the corporate culture. If you are in top management, others already think of you in this way. Be sure that you are living the vision every day, and when you stray from your chosen course, (and you will, because you're human), admit openly what happened and involve your teammates in developing plans to prevent similar occurrences. If you don't compromise your values for short-term financial results, you will be pouring the foundation upon which your organization can build for years to come. If you do go for short-term gain at the expense of the future, you send a troubling, mixed message to everyone in the company: "We have values in this company except when it comes to money. Then we'll do whatever we have to do to make the numbers." People will not rally around a corporate culture that lacks integrity and strength of character.

Some time ago, David Packard, co-founder of Hewlett Packard stated, in public, something to the effect that regardless of what the Wall Street analysts thought of his strategies, he was going to make decisions that were in the best *long-term* interest of his company. If they chose to criticize his strategies, thus reducing the short-term share value, they were welcome to do so, but he would no longer allow that to influence his business decisions. What a courageous thing to do and how totally appropriate! Unfortunately, many of the people in the financial community who evaluate corporate performance have never run anything bigger that a Lionel train and therefore do not have the knowledge base to support some of their pronouncements. Nevertheless, they continue to make them and we have allowed their opinions to influence how we operate our businesses. David Packard, for one, said enough is enough. That's leadership! That's being a steward of the corporate culture. Just take a look at what Hewlett Packard has accomplished in the last 20 years.

Now, I'm not suggesting that you put your business in jeopardy just to prove a point. From time to time, you may have to make decisions that fly in the face of what you believe and what you really would like to do. What I am suggesting is that, when these situations occur, you must explain the business realities to people in the organization and enlist their support for getting through the difficult time. People throughout organizations must learn the pragmatic realities of business if they are to make good decisions in their daily work. This learning includes the easy, fun things as well as the difficult.

Warning: If these exceptions become the rule, you have shot yourself in the foot. Be selective about how often and around what issues you must compromise. If you don't, it's sham and people will recognize it for what it is.

Coaching is another important skill for managers to learn. Most managers are so used to giving orders (no matter how well disguised they may be) that they have not learned true coaching skills. If you value the human resource for the leverage it can provide, you will surround yourself with the best talent you can find. You will have to pay for this talent but the return you will get from hiring the best and the brightest will far outweigh the additional expense of their compensation. *Remember, if you pay peanuts, you get monkeys.*

Coaching is different from directing in that you ask more than you tell. Accomplished coaches know the players well. They have hired the best they can find and have high expectations of them. However, circumstances change, things go wrong, and corrective action must be taken. When you hire the very best, you usually get people that are harder on themselves than you could ever be. That is how they got to be the very best. So, you frequently do not need to point out what they have done wrong, they are well ahead of you and already know. What you can do is ask them about their process. Phrases like, "Tell me how arrived at your decision" or, "What do you think we have learned from this experience and how do we do it more effectively next time?" and, "What resources do we have available to help us solve this problem?" are good coaching techniques. Remember, when you are coaching the best and brightest, the assumption is that they already "know" what to do. Our job is to help remove the obstacles that are preventing them from doing what they already know.

Be prepared to help when asked. From time to time, even the best get stuck and need advice. When people ask for help, you need to develop the skill to know when to ask a question and when to provide answers. There is no pat formula for this. It is an acquired skill and takes practice. You can really frustrate your people by continuing to ask questions when they are asking for help. You may indeed know the answer to their questions, and knowing when they actually need help as opposed to when they are just being lazy is an important attribute of a good coach. If you always answer people's questions for them when you are approached, you are setting yourself up for the trap of becoming an oracle.

While it may feel good to be asked for your knowledge, in general giving it does little or nothing to develop the people around you. If you always answer people's questions without first finding out what they already know and doing some coaching on how they could develop the knowledge for which they are searching, you are providing them with one of the best jobs in the company. You are doing all of their thinking and work, and they are collecting the paycheck. This being "all things to all people" in the company becomes the limiting factor in the growth and continued success of many organizations. When all roads lead through you, you become the problem, not the solution. Your job is to *prevent* people from coming to you for answers, and to ensure that they have the skills to solve business problems on their own.

"Human Behavior Specialist" or "Part-Time Psychologist" is another, and perhaps the most important, role for managers. Learning about human behavior (your own and that of others), may be the most powerful new skill you can develop. Good people "know" how to do their jobs. They frequently do not "behave" according to their knowledge. Like all humans, they behave according to what they believe, not what they know.

Developing the skills of facilitation, conflict resolution, and intervention can dramatically improve your effectiveness as a manager and, by extension, the performance of your organization. This is not to say that we are to turn our businesses into bastions of pop psychology. Quite the contrary. What I am suggesting is managers learn the pragmatic realities of why people behave the way they do and obtain the skills to facilitate a more appropriate pattern of behavior in the work place.

We will discuss more of the specifics of the psychological component of the managerial job in Chapters Five through Eight, which offers some tools to aid you in developing your knowledge base.

This new role may not seem as glamorous as the traditional role of manager but, in my experience, it is a much more fulfilling one. We are now defining the manager's job as "Resource Provider" and "Obstacle Remover." Imagine taking your current title off of your business card and replacing it with these designations. Hardly the image managers hold of themselves. After all, most went into management for the power, control, money, and recognition that went along with managerial jobs. Now these positions have become support to those who really run the business—the people closer to the customer.

Whether we like it or not, successful organizations are redefining the managerial job in these terms every day. The skills to become designers of organizations and processes, teachers and students, stewards of the corporate culture, coaches and human behavioral specialists are what is needed in business today.

Now let's turn our attention to the other side of the coin: the roles of the individual contributors in this new business paradigm.

CHAPTER FOUR

Redefining the Individual Contributor Role

Having paid a great deal of attention to how managers must change and grow, we must now equally emphasize the new roles and responsibilities of individual contributors in our organizations.

Managers and front-line workers alike have responded to the hierarchical model in largely the same fashion. Many workers feel they are powerless to impact the system in any meaningful way and, indeed, frequently feel victimized by the very organization that provides them employment. People show up every day, do their work at whatever level the are able to, and go home with little or no thought given to how they are doing the work or specifically how they could do it more effectively.

For individual contributors, the traditional charge has been to do what was assigned and to follow the rules. Remember; In orthodox organizations, management has all the power and does all the thinking. After decades of this overt and covert message, front-line workers at all levels have learned their roles and responsibilities.

The identifying categories "front-line worker" and "individual contributor" are meant to include positions from direct labor manufacturing to support staff to engineering or accounting or other professional jobs held by individuals in nonsupervisory, nonmanagerial slots. Education, compensation, or reporting relationships are unimportant when it comes to understanding the dynamic that exists in traditional business structures.

People who perceive themselves as having been victimized or somehow wronged by "the system" develop a set of strikingly similar biases that manifest in a predictable set of behaviors. These are what managers have to struggle with in transforming organizations. It is thus worthwhile to examine the reasons behind such behaviors.

First, recall that, prior to the construction of larger, hierarchical organizations, almost everyone was an individual contributor in the work place. The rewards of work went directly into the worker's pockets: There was linkage between what was produced and what was earned. This situation stimulated a natural incentive to produce higher quality work. With the advent of large, multilayer organizations, this linkage was lost. Combine that fact with the historical drumbeat that front-line workers were not to think about their work but merely do it and you begin to grasp the roots of the problems faced by many contemporary corporations.

For decades, we have sent a consistent message to our front-line workers, one that establishes them as second class citizens in our business enterprises and throughout society. A definite educational and cultural bias exists against people who work with their hands, perform repetitive work tasks, and hold nonmanagerial positions. Over the years, we have carved out some exceptions for our so-called "professional" positions, but they still do not hold the political and social stations that managers and, especially, executives enjoy. The most incompetent CEO is automatically assumed to be more valuable that the most skilled worker. We have placed different value on different job functions, further reinforcing the hierarchical model.

Of course, in the real world, we all know that the skill set required to run a company differs vastly from that required of a janitor—that is not my point. What is important to focus on is the social bias we have attached to each of these jobs. We immediately assume that the person running the company is better educated, smarter, and more valuable to society than the janitor. While in the great majority of cases, the educational part is correct, the level of intellect and value to society of the janitor may far exceed that of the CEO. Probably many would question the common sense and social value of someone like Charles Keating, who participated in the immense damage done to the Savings and Loan industry. Or, more recently, senior executives at Enron and WorldCom.

By attaching these biases to certain positions, we miss the opportunity to actually appreciate the individuals holding them. Through decades of this type of indirect, covert oppression, front-line workers have adapted readily—they have learned to mistrust, misinform, and even despise management. Not surprising when you view the world through their eyes. People are bright, adaptable creatures. Treat them like dogs for long enough and they will become those very dogs. Do it for decades, and they'll attack you!

It is also true that people become what management tells them to become. After all, management holds hire/fire power over them, and to many that power translates to a matter of life and death in their belief system: "If I lose my job, I won't be able to care for my family. We'll lose the house and the car. I won't be able to buy food and we will not survive." Now, this attitude may seem extreme, but the fear invoked by the prospect of losing one's job indeed conjures up thoughts quite similar to this.

Certainly, we will not be able to change decades (indeed centuries) of social bias in a few years. What we can do is begin to value the human resources in our businesses—one manager at a time, one worker at a time, one company at a time. Many workers are already well ahead of managers in their own lives. The manager's job is to recognize these trends and learn to capitalize on them. Actually, this is a great time to be in business—we have the opportunity to be wildly successful.

Let us now consider some of the challenges in transforming our organizations from the top down and the bottom up. Front-line workers will have to begin to examine their roles in the current dynamic existing in their organizations. In many cases, they are no more interested in doing this transformational work than the managers who are busy protecting *their* patch. Frequently, this is work that people avoid, partially because it can be difficult and painful and partially because they are just too "busy" to be bothered. Not many, regardless of the position they hold, will be at the head of the line volunteering to spearhead the process. Senior management, principally the CEO, will have to lead the charge.

In order to make the structural changes that you must to flatten your organization and make it more responsive to your customers, you must also address the new behaviors that are required to operate in the new model. These behaviors begin, for most front-line workers, with taking responsibility for themselves and their careers. As we discussed, businesses have operated in a paternalistic manner for decades and have bound their employees to them in unhealthy, dependent ways. We have disguised this dependency by calling it "employee loyalty," but it is in fact dependency. The *fact* is that people are free to leave their place of employment at any time to pursue a better situation for themselves. The *feelings* are that they cannot. They need the company for their survival. Remember that belief systems determine feelings, which in turn drive behaviors.

How many times have you, or others you observed, done something that seems to make no sense at all based on the data (facts) available? Investigation of these occurrences usually reveals that the individual involved was reacting to how they *felt* about the situation, not to what they *knew.*

Now, indeed, you may have implemented specific programs that bind employees to your organization financially; for instance, vested profit sharing, stock option plans that escalate with years of service, and/or employer-sponsored pension plans. These all serve to bind good employees to the company. Interestingly enough, they also bind unproductive employees in precisely the same way.

The changes you need to make in your organization may require fundamentally altering your entire concept of loyalty. Those already well down the road of organizational transformation have (not surprisingly) discovered that one of the causalities in the process was company loyalty. With all of the benefit-cutting, downsizing, reorganizing, out-sourcing, and other changes, people are scared to death. The fact is that many organizations can literally no longer afford to "take care" of their employees. The cost of providing robust employee benefit packages has become prohibitive. The practice of carrying marginal employees merely because they have been with the organization for a long period of time seems to be something business can no longer afford. Today, employees must earn their paycheck each day by their individual efforts.

In so-called "empowered" organizations, employee responsibility is a hallmark of the culture. It is no longer the responsibility of the employer to "take care" of the employees; rather, it is the employees' responsibility to take care of themselves. Whereas lifetime employment used to be the implied contract, you now find yourself dealing with the issue of individual employability. Where the company once took care of virtually all of the employees' insurance and financial needs, you now find individuals assuming more of this responsibility (some willingly and others kicking and screaming).

As with any major shift in our culture, there is good news and bad. The good news is that there has never been a more exciting and challenging time to be in business. Opportunities abound for people who can work independently and add value to their employer's business every day. The bad news (if you choose to call it bad) is that all employees must learn to take care of themselves and their families, and not depend on any one company to do it for them.

The ability to generate a decent living for themselves and their families is now squarely on the shoulders of each employee, regardless of his or her position, tenure, education, or political connections. I believe that over the long haul both employers and employees alike will benefit from this new work contract.

As employees must give up the illusion of security traditionally offered by employment (and it is an illusion), employers must stop complaining about the loss of loyalty from the work force and begin to engage them at a new level. Loyalty between employees and their employers still exists, but in a very different form. Blind loyalty is a thing of the past; mutual loyalty based on a complementary "work for compensation" agreement is the new reality.

Changing the belief systems of a major portion of the work force in terms of individual responsibility is a Herculean task. Nonetheless, this is where we must start. If people are not willing to take responsibility for their own lives, how can we reasonably expect them to take responsibility for their work and your businesses?

As with every major change, we must identify, once again, the WII FM (What's in it for me?) for all employees if we want them fully engaged. If people do not believe change is in their own best interest, they will resist and often refuse to acquire the new skills and adopt the new behaviors that are required. (Chapter Seven discusses some specific steps to test people's willingness and move them towards full enrollment in assuming responsibility for themselves.)

Once you have progressed beyond convincing your front-line workers that change is to their advantage, you can begin teaching them to become businesspeople. Your ultimate goal should be to turn all of your employees into businesspeople. In flatter, leaner organizations, people at all levels must develop the skills required to run the business. As "pay for performance" continues to become more commonplace, workers are having to discover what it takes to operate a financially successful business. In true pay-for-performance environments, people function as individual companies, working together in a collaborative fashion to achieve their individual as well as the company's collective goals. In essence, employees become Bob, Inc., Sue, Inc., Harry, Inc., and Jose, Inc. Each employee has his or her own individual profit and loss statement, which is directly affected by the job that they do for the company. In this environment, we re-establish the lost linkage between what we do and what we get.

An equally important element of this success formula is separating what we do from who we are, an internal dynamic at work in both front-line workers and managers. The psychology of image is universal and is not bound to education, position, or social station. Uniforms change but the behavior remains the same. Whether it is power ties, Armani suits, baseball caps, or jeans and T-Shirts, people all want to identify with some segment of society. A difficulty arises when people become so deeply attached to their internal image of themselves and what they represent that it often becomes extremely difficult for them to give up that attachment, even in favor of something better.

You see this phenomenon frequently when front-line workers are first promoted to a supervisory position. Their dress changes, their language changes, and, in some cases, their entire demeanor changes. During this transition, they are commonly rejected by their former peers and not yet accepted into the club by their new associates. This state of limbo has little to do with their skill set or qualifications for the position and everything to do with how "acceptable" they are deemed by their co-workers in both their former and new groups.

As organizations continue to evolve, more emphasis must be placed on such corporate cultural issues in order to reduce (and hopefully eliminate) the great majority of this "pigeonholing" that we practice. Each position in an organization serves an important function in the delivery of your products and/or services to your customers. Allowing "class bias" to exist in your company hampers your ability to meet and exceed customer expectations. Everyone in your organization must become involved in and dedicated to transforming the culture or you will never gain the leverage necessary to operate as a world-class company.

Once individual contributors have gotten the message that they are just as important to the success of the enterprise as other employees, they can begin to build their skill sets in those areas once strictly the territory of management. In flatter, team-based organizations, we need all the team members planning effectively, making good business decisions, and continuously improving their work products and processes. Individuals must learn to take risks, make decisions, and implement new methods without prior approval of management if these new structures are to survive.

I have seen too many restructurings abandoned when immediate results were not achieved. In almost every case, the behavioral and cultural issues in the organization were not addressed effectively, if at all. People require time to learn and adapt. Managers and front-line employees alike need to be intentional about learning new skills and practicing them in their everyday work situations. You need to create opportunities for learning and change and cause dialogue to occur throughout the process. This is work that may never be completed, but it needs to become standard business practice for all employees. Corporate culture ultimately should not be something we hire consultants to come in and "fix." If the skills do not exist in your organization to craft a well-designed transformation initiative, go get them. Whenever you can, rent them, don't buy them. This work should not be institutionalized in the Human Resources or any one department in the company. Make sure you are spending your resources wisely. Do not, under any circumstances, treat corporate cultural transformation as the project dejour.

In some reorganizations, the structure has been changed but, again, the cultural work has not been done. When results are not instantaneous, hierarchy begins to creep back in. Management positions are created to oversee the team models that are not yet working smoothly, sending yet another mixed message to the employees. Resources are expended in every area except those where the greatest return on investment lies: changing attitudes, belief systems and biases, and building new skills. Eventually, the new structure so resembles the old that people cannot tell the difference. A formal declaration is then made stating that the new model did not work and another reorganization will be required to get back to something workable. The bottom line is: *The implementation was flawed, but the system gets blamed.* Avoid "one shots"—they just do not work. Be certain you are in the transformation game for the long haul. Design processes and support systems that have plans covering years, not weeks.

Patience is vital to a successful transformation. Certainly, you should not have endless patience with those who refuse to join the game. Such people are obstructionist and must be reassigned or moved out, regardless of their level in the company or the amount of their individual contribution. If you tolerate aberrant behavior in your organization, it poisons the well.

Among your front-line workers, look for the natural leaders— they are there. Look for the people who are approached with questions and requests for help, for these are natural teachers and facilitators. Given their people skills and knowledge of human behavior, they may indeed be the best choice for a Team Leader position.

Begin to include increasing numbers of the work force in discussions of the financial performance of not only their work unit but the overall organization as well. Don't assume they wouldn't understand or care. You may be surprised at what they already know and how hungry they are to know more. You will likely discover people who are continuing their education on their own and who are already building the skills required to operate under the new rules. These people are not doing it because they have been told to do so, but because they are already motivated to improve themselves and curious to know more about how business works. You may find a budding accountant on the factory floor, a promising marketeer in the facilities department or your next salesperson, engineer, or technician in a clerical position in the office.

You may also learn that many of the people in your organization are proud of the positions they already hold and are primarily interested in honing their skills in that particular area of expertise. Think about the possibility of having people who are genuinely interested in doing their particular job. Having the best receptionist in your industry may bring your company more business that hiring another three salespeople. Remember, we create what we believe. If you still hear yourself thinking things like, "Oh, she's just the receptionist" or, "He's only a factory worker," *you* are part of the problem. If a holder of one of those positions believes the same thing, *he or she is the problem* because such thought is terribly self-limiting.

At a management retreat I facilitated for one of my clients in a petroleum-related business, there was a fair amount of grousing about the "workers' attitudes and management's seeming inability to get them to do what they wanted. Responding to this under-current, I altered the agenda and had the managers do the following exercise:

Take a piece of paper and draw a line down the middle from top to bottom. At the top of the left-hand column, write the word "salaried." At the top of the right-hand column, write the word "hourly." Then, for the next 90 seconds, write all of the one-word descriptors or adjectives that come to mind for the "salaried" people in your company. At the end of the 90-second period, stop and then repeat the process for the "hourly" people.

Next, I had each of the executives read aloud their descriptors, first for the "salaried" employees and then for the "hourly" people. The results were absolutely staggering. The lists from most of the group for the salaried people included such descriptors as "educated," "honest," "hard working," "dedicated," "creative," "intelligent," and so on. On the hourly side of the ledger were descriptors such as "thief," "lazy," "stupid," "hair ball," "dirt bag" and, well, you get the drift. The group was embarrassed and somewhat shocked to discover how each of them truly perceived their co-workers. I then posed the following question to the group. "Do you guys think, for one minute, that by holding those beliefs, you are not at least partially responsible for creating that reality back at your place of business when you go to work each day?" The room was silent, a few jaws dropped and no more needed to be said. We then set about the task of crafting initiatives that would help the executive staff change their obvious, negative bias about their hourly workers.

My experience has been that organizations are populated with bright, well-intentioned, capable people and that the only thing between where we are now and how good we could really be is *us*. Not just management, but the great majority of people in most organizations. A respected colleague of mine recently said to me, "On a scale of 1 to 10, I am about a 3 on my better days compared to what I could be if I could only get out of my own way." That statement really had an impact on me. It brought into clear focus how much of our human potential is wasted fussing with stuff that has little or nothing to do with what we are capable of.

As you begin to view your entire labor force in a different light, you will have to rethink many of the developmental needs of your staff. Traditionally, we have provided mostly technical training for individual contributors and reserved managerial development for people currently holding such positions or occasionally for someone who is being groomed for management. Now we must begin to develop what were traditionally "management skills" in the entire work force.

In flatter, team-based organizations, individual contributors will have to develop skills in many areas that heretofore did not concern them. Communication skills are paramount to operating in a team environment. In a command-and-control structure, people had to understand how to take orders and perform tasks, but not necessarily how to communicate effectively. As front-line workers are charged with making more decisions and having greater control over their work and environment, their ability to communicate their status to others both verbally and in writing becomes critical.

Most organizations are more accustomed to having managers and supervisors locate the information required, design and generate reports, and literally bear the burden for the great majority of information flow in the company. In flatter organizations, there simply are not enough people to operate in this manner. Many staff positions and management jobs have been eliminated, and in the vast majority of situations I encounter, those who remain (the survivors) usually have not had sufficient training or experience to take up the slack. Hence, we witness the resultant chaos currently being experienced by many organizations following an internal restructuring. Re-engineering addresses the structural needs of the organization and the better-designed initiatives also identify training needs for the people involved. What they almost always miss is the behavioral changes required to take advantage of the training and new opportunities. Remember our mantra: If people do not "believe" it is in their own best interest to learn and change, they simply will not do so.

Another major area for new learning for the front-line workers is planning. When management did virtually all the planning, it eliminated the need for front-line workers to think in either a strategic or tactical manner about their work. They simply did what they were told, when they were told. Again, in flatter organizations, many of the people who used to do the telling are no longer around; consequently, workers at all levels are having to develop skills in how to plan for both the short and long term.

Due to the rate of change in the world today, planning has become much more of a daily work process and less of an annual event. While strategic, long-range, and annual operating plans still have value and need to be done, it is at the implementation level where planning determines your ultimate success. The best strategic plan, poorly implemented, is not significantly better than no plan at all. People throughout organizations must develop the capacity to plan their work and work their plan. They must become skilled at anticipating changes and problems. They must also develop the related skills to react to the things they cannot anticipate, and control those which they can. Your job, as managers, is to provide the infrastructure and many of the opportunities for individual contributors to learn these new skills. Continuous learning *must* become a condition of employment for all employees.

As a subset of the planning function, goal-setting and measurement are key to the success of any work team. Team members and team leaders must be skilled in setting meaningful, short-and long-term goals and tracking progress towards those goals. There are any number of quality goal-setting and tracking systems available in the training realm. What is important is not which one you select but, again, how you implement them. Any goal-setting and tracking system worth its salt requires a high degree of integrity in its design and execution. Things like articulating specific criteria for goals, frequency and format of team meetings, and quality of corrective action when goals are not achieved are important characteristics of any effective goal-based methodology.

Goal-based systems by their very construct invite accountability. They have built in peer pressure and can be used to help teams become increasingly effective. Like any other tool, however, they can be used in inappropriate ways. If you use the wrong end of a screwdriver, you're going to hurt yourself!

A goal-based system should never be used as a means to "set up" employees performing poorly, embarrass anyone, or beat anyone over the head. They are intended to be used as positive tools to improve productivity and overall performance. The primary difference between an effective system and one that does not provide positive return on investment is how they are implemented from the beginning. You must be setting goals around those business factors that are vital to each particular work team. Goal accomplishment should be rewarded and positive coaching should accompany goal failure.

Interestingly enough, the managerial function of staffing also becomes critical to individual contributors in team structures. As self-managed work teams continue to grow in popularity, individual team members need to acquire the skills related to recruiting, interviewing, selecting, and retaining employees, as well as participating in 360-degree feedback and peer review sessions. Once considered to be a "behind closed door" function between the hiring manager and human resources, staffing is becoming normalized as yet one more daily business practice at which many must become proficient.

When you consider a true team environment, it makes sense for individual team members to be involved in the selection, appraisal and ongoing coaching of their fellow team members. Everyone must become a talent scout. Team leaders may assume more of a leadership role in this function. However, leaving these duties solely to team leaders smacks of hierarchy and affords you the opportunity to fall back into old behaviors by loading too much onto the team leaders and allowing other team members to depend on them for much of the work. This is where the art of inquiry can be most helpful. Effective coaching and counseling requires asking good questions. The ability to inquire without causing polarization facilitates positive, creative solutions to problems.

Facilitation skills is another area in which all your employees should learn to excel. As employees move from job to job within a given company or between companies, they must deal with a wide range of personalities and skill sets. Becoming skilled at facilitating groups of people in resolving problems, planning, and other areas of work is essential to continued success. Effective facilitation requires a deep understanding of, and appreciation for, the differences between people and business situations. Facilitation is not about right and wrong, and most certainly is not about your opinion if you are doing the facilitating.

Quite often, in my managerial career, I would ask another employee who possessed good facilitation skills to chair a problem-solving meeting where I felt my best contribution was at the problem-solving level. Managers or front-line workers who attempt to both do the work and facilitate the group simultaneously are looking for trouble. Usually you end up doing a marginal job in both areas. In situations where several "levels" are represented, it is often the best course for the most senior person in the room not to facilitate. Remember, if you are the senior person in the room, always be the last person to speak on any issue, not the first. If you speak first, you are in danger of biasing the group towards your point of view, simply because you are the boss. All too often I participate in meetings where the senior person begins with, "Here's what I think. What do you guys think?" You can just see people going through some internal version of "Oh, I think what you think, boss." What comes out of their mouths may not be these words exactly, but unless you have an exceptionally strong group, you will not get the best of their thinking when you as the most senior authority are the first to speak.

Finally, leadership is a skill each and every employee must build. In team-based structures, we depend on people acting courageously. When I say "leadership," I am not necessarily referring to what is commonly known as heroic leadership, but rather to a pattern of behavior that reinforces a common set of values expressed by the majority of employees.

Leadership involves pointing out the uncomfortable issues that you may naturally want to duck and *doing* something about them. Leadership involves making the unpopular decisions when it is in the best interest of the business. Leadership involves challenging colleagues on inappropriate behavior and providing counseling where necessary. Leadership also involves having the ability to *receive* coaching and counseling from one's co-workers.

If you desire to increase your leadership skills, there are a number of things you can do. First, you must assume the leadership position. Be alert for opportunities to lead. Be active and participative in your work group and others—don't wait to be asked. Natural leaders know this intuitively, whereas others must acquire the skills by practicing.

Next, be willing to assume the risks. Leadership is by definition a risky position. Leaders are usually the first to get the credit and always the first to get the blame. Be bold, stand by your convictions and don't compromise your values. Now, let's be clear about the risks. The great majority of business situations do not involve life-and-death issues, so what are the real risks? In most cases, the risk is that of being wrong and getting the blame for it. This is risky at the feeling level but seldom has a major impact on one's career (unless mistake-ridden risk taking is a pattern for you).

Mistakes are part of the normal business process in any healthy organization and, as previously mentioned, are opportunities for coaching. All too often, managers will treat a mistake as if it is the end of the world. Many managers are deadly serious about businesses. Every situation is treated as a life and death catastrophe. Grim faces with furrowed brows promote a highly stressful atmosphere where employees work in fear of making the next mistake and incurring the wrath of management.

This inability to lighten up and have some fun has a price attached to it. If creating anxiety is a major theme in your organization, people will begin to fear the environment, and the worksite will become a pretty dismal place. I routinely tell my clients, "Lighten up. This is not Middle East peace. Nobody dies." Now, when I'm working in health care delivery organizations, I do not use this line because in their environment, people really do die. Fortunately for the great majority of you, the stakes are not that high.

Leadership requires perspective about what is going on in the business. When things go wrong (and they will), don't look for someone to blame, look for a solution to the problem and then go back and learn what you can from the experience. This is where systems thinking is so important. When we continually react at the symptomatic level, we are doomed to fixing the same problems over and over again. When we deal with things at the systematic level, we can craft solutions that last.

Leadership is primarily an attitude. If you maintain a positive attitude that does not comprehend blame, you will have an enormous impact on the people around you. For reasons unknown to me, people have a great affinity for complaining. People seem to love to get together and gripe about the boss, the company, and their general lot in life. While there is usually some short-term gratification in this "venting," it does little good for the group or the organization and, if allowed to exist as a norm, can destroy a culture.

Genuine leaders do not participate in these kinds of activities. They know that their energies are better spent on making a positive contribution to the organization. Such leaders not only refuse to participate in destructive negativity, they encourage their co-workers to do the same.

These changing roles for managers and front-line workers can be extremely unsettling for many, as both groups are redefining themselves and their positions in the organization and are seeking new identities.

It is important to note that even in team-based organizations, managers and executives are still "in charge." What has changed is the definition of what being "in charge" means. In my client work, from time to time, I will ask a team to think about a cruise ship company and the various roles that are played by all those involved in the enterprise. In this exercise, I ask, "Which job would you like with the cruise ship company?" Some reply "captain", others say "navigator", still others want to be "chief engineer" or "recreational director", or "purser" or a myriad of yet other functions. The one job seldom, if ever, chosen is that of the designer of the ship itself. But designer is precisely the new job description for managers. We must become designers of organizations and processes, facilitators of dialogue, and stewards of the culture.

PART TWO

Tools for Handling Transformation

CHAPTER FIVE

Transforming Your Organization:
Begin With Yourself

Given the weight of the historical influences that have shaped current labor-management relations in America, it sometimes seems virtually impossible for modern managers to actually change their own attitudes and beliefs, never mind those of others. When you are faced with the day-to-day pressures of managing your organization, making time for issues of the magnitude of cognitive change frequently takes a back seat to the pressures of the daily routine. Executives and managers often feel ill-equipped to begin the journey or have been unsuccessful in previous attempts, and are reticent to pursue yet one more initiative.

In light of the realities of the task, these feelings are understandable, but if we are to genuinely transform our organizations, we must begin with ourselves. Much of the initial work suggested here involves solitary pursuits. Self-examination is always a difficult and, more often than not, a painful process. Nonetheless, it is a rich and largely untapped area where advantageous leverage for businesses lies. Be prepared to struggle with the start-up process. Be aware of your own natural resistance to change. Spend time with yourself preparing for the process. Realize at the internal, emotional level that you are embarking on a long journey. This is a marathon, not a hundred-yard dash. Indeed, for many, this process becomes a veritable life's work.

In this chapter and those that follow, you will encounter a series of tools to aid you in your own personal transformation and that of your organization. The process described has been sequenced with care and while, as I have said, there is no single solution to these complex issues, you may find it helpful to follow these broad guidelines. The tools will be applied in various ways with differing levels of success and will be operating on various levels. This is a normal artifact of the transformation process. While these tools have been "field tested" in many organizations, and in many ways are tried and true, their application requires some learning and skill to gain maximum benefit.

The tools are categorized in four broad areas: appraisals, personal instruments, surveys/data gathering, and behavioral/experiential instruments. Each is designed to provide you with specific data and knowledge of how to more effectively integrate people with the organization.

The first step is to examine where and how you spend your time at work. This step is rudimentary, but do not dismiss it, for it is extremely consequential. Many of us are not aware of where our time really goes during our work day. When we consider taking on new duties or tasks, frequently our first thought is, "How am I going to find the time for this? I'm already overloaded as it is." While such may be the case, it is important to analyze where and how your hours are being spent. Are you spending your time on the issues that are truly vital to your business or are you merely practicing the habits that you have developed over the years? Are you spending your time on the familiar or are you mentally stretching yourself, continually honing your skills? Remember, you can never *find* time for anything, you've got to *make* time.

This exercise begins with the realization that time is our most precious asset. Time, in fact, may be the only nonrenewable resource that exists. You can lose your wallet or car keys and possibly get them back. You may even lose your mind and be able to get that back, but once you've lost time, it is gone forever. When you have actually acknowledged how valuable *your* time really is, you are ready to begin the process of allocating it to the activities that will bring you and your organization the greatest return on investment. That is why the little time it takes you to follow through here is well worth the effort.

Begin by estimating the allocation of your time at work. The chart you see on page 79 is an example of a typical Time Estimation

Form. Photocopy it for use. In the left-hand column, list the activities where you believe the majority of your time is currently being spent. In the right-hand column, estimate the hours of your total time actually spent at those activities during a typical work week. The numbers will give you an overview of where you believe your time is going.

Estimate of Work Time

Activity	Hours of total time
1	
2	
3	
4	
5	
6	
7	
8	
9	
10	
TOTALS	

Once you have *estimated* your time spent, the next step is to track and record where your time is *actually* being spent. Photocopy and use the Time-Tracking Form on page 80 for a two-week period, recording your time twice daily, at noon and at the end of the work day. An easy method for recording where your time actually goes is to create a legend that corresponds to your activities and use a simple check mark system, with each check mark representing 1/2 hour. Twice a day—at noon and at quitting time—enter a check mark in the corresponding box for every 1/2 hour spent on each designated activity.

Time—Tracking Form

ACTIVITY	M	T	W	T	F	S	S
1							
2							
3							
4							
5							
6							
7							
8							
9							
10							

Sample legend:

1. Planning

2. 1 on 1 Coaching

3. Meetings

4. Telephone

5. Drive Time

6. Administrative

7. Customer Contact

8. Fire Fighting

9. Responding to Others

10. Learning

$\sqrt{}$ = 1/2 Hour

After two weeks of tracking and recording your time, compare your actual time spent with your original estimate on the Estimate of Work Time Form (p. 79), analyze where your hours have actually been spent, and decide what changes you would like to make in these patterns. (One of the more vital changes you *can* make is to find time for learning.) When you have decided on changes, set goals over the next two weeks for implementing them. Continue to track and record your time and compare your new habits to the goals you set for their activation. See how close you came to achieving your new time goals and reflect on what you have gained from the experience.

The effort required for this considered review of work time pays off. Many who have done it have experienced enormous productivity gains. Remember, one of the crucial aims we have here is *making* the time in our work schedules to devote to our personal learning, so we can begin the process of transforming our organizations into the energized, competitive enterprises that they must become in order to survive and prosper.

Once you have allotted time in your schedule to devote to new endeavors, do an inventory of your personal skill set. Answering the questions in the Personal Skill Inventory below will give you some of the information that you will need to begin re-tooling your skills.

PERSONAL SKILL INVENTORY

1. List your formal educational credentials.

2. What are your major continuing education accomplishments?

3. Do you think that your current level of knowledge is sufficient to carry you through the end of your career?
   Yes_____No_____

   Exlain: _____

4. What additional knowledge do you believe you need to ensure continued success in your career?

5. What specific things have you done in the last three years to build your base of knowledge?

6. What is your plan for building your base of knowledge over the next three years?

7. Do you intend to hold a position similar to your current one three years from now?
    Yes_____No_____

8. If yes, what specific knowledge do you need to acquire in order to remain in a similar position?

9. If no, what type of position would you like to hold three years from now?

10. What specific knowledge do you need to acquire in order to obtain such a position?

11. How has your industry and/or profession changed since you began working in it?

12. What, in your current skill/knowledge base, do you feel is transferable to other industries and/or professions?

    Explain: _____

13. What are the last three books you have read related to your personal/professional skill development?

    What did you learn from this reading?_____
    _____

14. How do you see your current job changing over the next three years?

15. How do you see your industry/profession changing over the next three years?

16. How do you see the world changing over the next three years?

Upon completing the Personal Skill Inventory, you may discover that you haven't done much in terms of learning in the last few years or that what you have learned is strictly related to the technical aspects of your job. Let's be clear: Management is a *people* business, not a *thing* business. If you have not already done so, begin to build your knowledge base in the areas of human behavior and organizational development. This book is a good start. Read everything that you can get your hands on concerning this subject. Read about organizational transformations in your own industry and those outside of it. Find out what the leading edge, successful corporations are doing. Build your network of contacts. Learn from the successes and failures of others. Use your newly created time to learn what you need. If you find reading burdensome, subscribe to an audio tape service, rent video tapes, attend seminars and workshops, but whatever you do, learn, learn, learn.

Books highly recommended are:

* *The Fifth Discipline* by Peter Senge (Doubleday/Currency, 1990)
* *Stewardship* by Peter Block (Berett-Koehler, 1993)
* *The 7 Habits of Highly Successful People* by Stephen Covey (Fireside, Simon & Schuster, 1989)
* *Creating The High Performance Team* by Steve Buchhloz and Thomas Roth (John Wiley & Sons, Inc., 1987)
* *Organizational Learning: A Theory Of Action Perspective* by Chris Argyris Addison-Wesley, 1978)

All are credible works and can greatly enhance your knowledge of things you can do in your own organization.

If your reading list seems oppressive, subscribe to services such as Soundview's Executive Book Summaries* or Audio-Tech Business Book Summaries. These truncated versions of the latest management books and audio programs can greatly reduce the amount of your reading time.

In the work place, be public about your passion for learning. Challenge others in the organization to follow your lead. Infect your company with the learning virus. Make continuous learning an integral part of your corporate culture. Ultimately, make it a condition of employment in your business.

Once you have established your own pattern of continuous learning, begin sharing more of your knowledge with colleagues. Institute a "book of the month" assignment in various work teams and organize discussions. Find out *what* people are learning and *how* they are applying the knowledge. Begin a serious dialog about what other organizations are doing and how your business stacks up. Engage your colleagues. Discover what they know and believe, and share that information with others in the company. In short, learn and teach, continuously.

Experiment with organizational structures and work processes and find out what is worth changing. Follow the direction implied in Robert Krigel's best-selling book titled *If It Ain't Broken—Break It* (Warner Books, 1992). Be bold, this is no time for timidity. Don't worry so much about making mistakes. Make decisions. If they are less than perfect, you can change them. Become an agent for change in your organization. Stir the pot—you may be delighted with the results.

All this learning and sharing of information takes time, but must become part of your normal business procedure. Remember, you may have to change *your* behavior first to begin the process of

---

*   Soundview Executive Book Summaries, 5 Main Street, Bristol, Vt. 05443-1398; Telephone: 1-800/521-1227. Audio-Tech Business Book Summaries, 117 W. Harrison Bldg., 6th Floor, Suite A-461, Chicago, Il. 60605. Telephone 1-800/776-1910.

helping others change theirs. Development of our skills and the skills of those around us is becoming mandatory to the success of any manager or executive in today's ever-changing business environment.

As you change some of your old habits, those around you may begin to wonder what's going on. If they notice, that's good news. It means they're paying attention and that's important. Every time someone notices and asks, treat that moment as a sales opportunity. Sell the merits of continuous learning, actively. Promote your new direction with enthusiasm. If we are not committed to our own self development, how can we expect our employees to be committed to theirs?

Early in my career, the first sales manager I had taught me one of the most important lessons in my professional development. He told me that a sale takes place, "when there is a transfer of enthusiasm." This simple message has stayed with me all these years and I have seen it played out in every possible business situation. After all, we're always selling something—thoughts, ideas, concepts, products, services, etc. If I can get you as excited about my idea, product, or service as I am, I've got you. This is the essence of the transfer of enthusiasm. Continuous learning and organizational transformation are no different. People have to emotionally embrace things (as well as intellectually understand them) in order to accept them fully.

So create an energized atmosphere in your organization. Sell this era of rapid continuous change as a great opportunity. Stop complaining about how hard everything is and get on with the job of mastering your craft. Accept that your job is changing and that we all will need different skills to manage in the new paradigms. Don't worry if you haven't got all the answers, you'll discover together what needs to be done.

When I think about learning and reflect on my days in school, the teachers that had the greatest impact on me were not necessarily those who had the best grasp of the subject matter, but rather those who had a true passion for learning. They would come into the classroom alive with the electricity of a new discovery. Their energy and enthusiasm was contagious. It inspired me to learn along with them. The same can be true in your business. We must create such an atmosphere—it is our job.

Initially, others may not share your excitement for new directions, and may even resist, openly or subversively. Don't be discouraged by this, it's normal. Seek out those in the organization who have a passion for learning. Partner with them in visible endeavors. Slowly but steadily broadcast the message that this is the future direction of the company. Ultimately, people will either get it and get on board or they will leave for a situation that they deem to be safer and not as stressful. (When they find it, I sure would like to know where it is, because such situations are rapidly becoming extinct.)

Once you have established continuous learning as the new norm in your business, it is time for a bit more structured approach to organizational transformation. With all of the fear and doubt in people's minds these days, it is important to recognize that a host of barriers to any change effort exists. People have become emotionally vested in their positions in organizations and, over the years, many have attached much of their self worth to what they do for a living. In other words, people equate who they are with what they do: "I am what's printed on my business card." This belief in "I am what I do" causes people to perceive any change or inferred change to what they do as a threat to themselves as individuals. These threats are met by a variety of responses, from passive-aggressive foot dragging to open hostility (which can include litigation.)

Managing these fears and the resulting reactions is a tricky business that involves skills many managers and executives have not spent much time developing. These skills include positive confrontation, facilitation, true win-win negotiating, and group dynamic management. Engaging people in our business enterprises requires a different kind of buy-in, for different reasons, with different outcomes and expectations. Engaging people at the emotional level requires reaching them in ways different from those we have traditionally considered.

The information on how to involve people and how to get the true buy-in that we seek is, as previously mentioned, available to everyone on the most listened to radio station in the world. Everyone listens to it every day of their lives: It's WII FM—WHAT'S IN IT FOR ME. If you can connect with the "what's in it for me" element in others, you stand a good chance of winning them over. If, as employers, we can ascertain what individuals really want in their lives and play a role in providing some of those things, we can truly enlist people in a way that will allow them to participate at a much higher level. Once you have achieved this alignment, individuals begin to see themselves as contributing directly to their own lives and not feeling that they are merely breaking their backs for some faceless corporation. At this point, we move beyond just money.

With the time that you have gained and the atmosphere of continuous learning that you have established from applying the guides of the first two steps, you are ready to blend in additional specifics. Now start to engage your team members in crafting their own personal vision statements. This process can be difficult and, in many organizations, is truly counter cultural. Personal vision statements are just that. They are personal. Generally, they do not involve the employer directly. They are crafted by individual members of teams who usually involve their families in creating these statements.

In order to transform an organization, it is vital that this personal vision process begin with the CEO and the executive team. In large organizations, accomplishing it at the departmental level has some impact and is certainly worth doing, but if you want to change the culture, it must start at the top.

To begin, it is sometimes helpful to gather some data on things that are really important to you. The Life Satisfaction Index (p. 89) is a simple rating instrument that may assist you in collecting this data. Read each statement, and then rate yourself on a scale of 1 to 100 as to what you would like or where you currently are. After completing the ratings, total your scores in the area provided. Low scores indicate either a low area of interest or a low satisfaction level around those issues in your life. A high score indicates the opposite. Only you can decide if the scores are areas of satisfaction or dissatisfaction or simply an area of little interest to you. This exercise is intended only to give you some data about how you feel in relationship to various aspects of your life.

LIFE SATISFACTION INDEX

AREA   *RATING (1-100)*

1. Have a variety of close friends   _____

2. Spend time alone thinking,   _____
    meditating, or praying

3. Exercise vigorously   _____

4. Have adequate quality and quantity   _____
    time spent with family

5. Have a job that pays well   _____

6. Am already engaged in the career that I want   _____

7. Am involved in community activities   _____

8. Enjoy reading and do so   _____

9. Spend time I want doing the things I want   _____

10. Am at peace with my chosen religion   _____

11. Eat nutritious, well-balanced meals   _____

12. Write or call members of the family   _____

13. Am creating an adequate retirement fund   _____

14. See opportunities for advancement
    in my career   _____

15. Belong to associations within the community   _____

16. Am mentally challenged in life   _____

17. Have a fulfilled social life   _____

18. Attend religious services   _____

19. Am involved in sports regularly   _____

20. Spend time I want with family   _____

21. Have substantial savings account   _____

22. Am really good at and enjoy my work   _____

23. Give back to the community   _____

24. Like to go to museums, fairs, libraries, etc.   _____
    to see what's new

SCORING YOUR ANSWERS

(Photocopy and complete)

Place the rating number for each answer opposite the statement number below and total them.

Social/Personal	Spiritual	Physical	Family
1. _____	2. _____	3. _____	4. _____
9. _____	10. _____	11. _____	12. _____
17. _____	18. _____	19. _____	20. _____
_____	_____	_____	_____
TOTAL	TOTAL	TOTAL	TOTAL

Financial	Professional	Community	Mental
5. _____	6. _____	7. _____	8. _____
13. _____	14. _____	15. _____	16. _____
21. _____	22. _____	23. _____	24. _____
_____	_____	_____	_____
TOTAL	TOTAL	TOTAL	TOTAL

Now that you have completed your Life Satisfaction Index, you are ready to begin crafting your Personal Vision Statement. The following suggestions are designed to aid you. This endeavor may be one of the most important in your career. Please give it the time and attention that it deserves. Please give yourself the time and attention that *you* deserve.

Begin by going to a place of quiet and serenity that has special meaning for you. It could be your favorite fishing spot, a favorite room of the house, or any other location where you feel comfortable and will not be interrupted. Some people find it helpful to have some relaxing music playing, while others prefer silence for this portion of the journey. Most importantly, give yourself a block of uninterrupted time. At least one hour with no visitors, telephone calls, pagers, or other distractions.

Start by just letting your mind go quiet. Practice noticing the "mind buzz" that seems to accompany us all in the very busy and complex lives that we lead. Do your best to relax and let go of the tensions of the day. Notice how "busy" you really are and let this pass.

When you are sufficiently relaxed and centered, begin to generate a few ideas about what you want out of your life. Jot them down on a piece of paper or in a notebook. Remember that no one else will see them. This list is between you and you. There is no "right" way to go about this so be careful not to spend a lot of time trying to "figure out" your vision, but rather pay attention to those things that mean the most to you in your life.

Imagine achieving the things that are most important to you in your life. How would it be to have the perfect job or to live in the perfect house in the perfect area or to have the optimum relationships? How would it feel, what would you gain? Avoid the natural self-limiting thoughts such as "that's impossible" or "I couldn't possibly have everything that I want."

As these images begin to crystallize in your mind, continue listing them. Pay attention to things like how it feels, what it looks like, how you would describe it to others. Complete this step by doing a summary of what it is that you want most and what you would have when you achieved these results.

Next, reflect on what you have listed. Did you discover anything? Were your answers close to what you already knew you wanted or did new ideas and concepts surface? Did you find the self-encounter difficult? It commonly is. Much of our early training makes it tough if not impossible for us to imagine having everything that we really want. Our parents, as well as our religious and educational systems, often tend to view this kind of thinking as selfish, as opposed to self-centered in a positive way.

In compiling your lists, you may have experienced any number of self-limiting phrases generating from your own mind. Stuff such as "No way am I going to have what I really want" or, "It doesn't really matter what I want." These and other well-entrenched belief systems tend to undermine our ability to achieve. They actually have little to do with our capabilities or even with opportunities that present themselves but are, rather, no more than attitudes concerning our perceptions of what we deserve. You might also, during this exercise, have found yourself considering what other family members may want or what is expected of you by society due to your position in life, be it mother, father, business executive, community leader, or whatever. You may even have experienced *not knowing* what you want or, in some cases, being frightened by what you envisioned.

Remember, this listing activity is just a thought experiment. We do not necessarily have to act on what we create, and we may well want to consciously delineate boundaries for our visions.

Another mental "yeah, but" that surfaces is something on the order of "I know what I want, but I can't get it at work." Some people feel that their personal vision is not at all compatible with what they think their employer would tolerate, so they deem it to be ludicrous to even consider a personal vision. At this point in the process, such thoughts and others we have mentioned are natural roadblocks that should be dismissed as so much "mind buzz." What we *believe* to be possible is not important; rather, what is crucial is *what we really want.* The difference between these mental sets is great.

After you have considered what you have listed and studied it, you may feel the need to modify or form your vision at this time. This desire commonly occurs, and you should feel free to apply it.

Having fashioned a Personal Vision Statement that "feels" right, return now to your Life Satisfaction Index scores and ask yourself the question, "How does my vision match those areas in my life that I believe to be important?" Compare your personal vision to your scores in each category and ask yourself the following questions.

Social/Personal	What personal characteristics would I like to exhibit in my life? What do I want my social relationships to be like?
Spiritual	What purpose am I to fulfill in life? What specific activities do I engage in to nourish my spirit?
Physical	How do I view my physical health? What do I need to do to maintain a healthy body?
Family	What types of relationships do I want with my family members?
Financial	What material things do I want to own? How much money do I need? How will I know when enough is enough?

Professional	What is my ideal professional situation? What impact would I like my career to have on others?
Community	What is my vision for the community I live and work in? What are my roles and responsibilities in that community?
Mental	How do I view my own mental development? What am I doing to build my intellectual skills and keep myself current?

Now, revisit your vision statement in light of these questions and again rewrite as you deem necessary. Remember, for now, you are creating a Personal Vision Statement *just for yourself*, which you may or may not choose to share with others. Don't be bashful about listing anything that seems to have value to you. There are no right or wrong desires here.

At this point, it is valuable to test what you have created against some standard questions. Your vision statement probably consists of a combination of both selfless and self-centered elements. Ask yourself the following questions about each item in your vision.

If I could create it today, would I ?

You may answer "yes" immediately to many elements of your vision, while others may not pass this test. Still others will get a qualified "yes." Many visions in their early stages are incomplete or fuzzy in their definitions and will be clarified through this process. For example, you may have created a vision that has you living in the south of France on the beach and while, in reality that may be great for a vacation, you may not actually want to live there. Things like distance from family members and friends, language barriers, and citizenship may make a vision like this somewhat impractical or actually undesirable when subjected to close examination.

If I had it now, what would that give me?

This is where we zero in on WII FM—What's In It For Me? Many people say they want one thing or another, but what they are actually asking for is a symbol of their true desires. For example, people may indicate they want motorcycles or sailboats when what they are actually seeking in their lives is a sense of freedom. Others will maintain they want power and position when what they are really after is recognition and adulation. Let's be clear: Some people genuinely *do* want the sailboat, and there is absolutely nothing wrong with that. The value lies in each individual discovering what is personally important and beginning to manage life toward achieving those elements of their vision.

Throughout this process, continue to compare what you have listed against what you really want. For example, part of your vision may deal with money. You may say that you want to make more money. If that is the case, test that assumption by asking yourself the question, "If I had more money, what would that do for me?" You might answer, "I could buy that sailboat I have always wanted." If that is your answer, ask, "Assume that I have the sailboat, what would that do for me?" A possible answer might be, "I could spend more time alone relaxing." Continue to ask what that would do for you until you are convinced that your vision actually represents what you basically want, and does not consist merely of symbols of what you want.

When you have completed your Personal Vision Statement, make it presentable by typing or printing it in a form that allows you to reference it easily and to share it with others.

Now is the time to introduce your newfound vision to your family or close friends, certainly not as some kind of ultimatum but, rather, as a sharing of some of your more intimate hopes and dreams. All families have certain pragmatic requirements: house payments, car payments, college expenses, and so on. While these may indeed be current realities, so too are our hopes and dreams. Many executives, upon scrutinizing what they really want, have chosen to change their life style in order to gain better inner balance and more fulfillment. Make this sharing fun. It should be taken as an adventure into your creativity. Talk about the things in your current life style that you would not want to change and those that you would if you could find a way. Explain that your plans are to enter into a new kind of partnership with your company, one differing from the past, one that will result in you getting more of the things in your life that are fundamentally important to you.

You may find that after sharing your vision with your family or friends, you might decide to yet again modify your Personal Vision Statement. This should be done to enhance the vision and not be a retreat into your current situation. Bear in mind that we create reality by what we know, what we believe, and what we are willing to do about it.

The following is an example of a Personal Vision Statement. As mentioned previously, there is no "right" way to fashion a vision statement, so take care not to follow the example too closely. Remember, this is *your* personal vision.

Sample Personal Vision Statement

My vision is to live my life with intentional balance between my physical, emotional, and spiritual selves. My career success will be measured by the creation of personal net worth affording me a passive income of $150,000 per year (in today's dollars) by the time I reach age 55.

My personal success will be measured by the honest, loving manner in which I function with my family, friends, and colleagues.

I will maintain dual residences, one favoring summer and the other winter and will work outside the traditional corporate structure in a consulting or teaching role. This new role will provide me with the flexibility to travel, study, and enjoy my friends and extended family to the fullest.

The next thing to do is to share your experience with your team at work. You may not yet be comfortable in sharing your actual vision with your colleagues at this time. If so, then consider sharing the fact that you actually did formalize one, as well as some thoughts and feelings about the process. In so doing, you begin to interest your team members in undertaking the exercise themselves. As the president or CEO, encourage each member of your executive team to go through the same vision-creating process you did yourself. The ultimate goal is to have each team member create their own Personal Vision Statement and share the specifics with every other member of the team.

This whole process can be seen as everything from a lunatic waste of time to an invasion of privacy so proceed slowly, with caution. Your intent is not to annoy or anger your team but to open communications around people's most heartfelt issues and to thereby build trust in the team. What you are looking for here is an honest sharing of people's dreams and, consequently, those things that motivate them at a primal level.

A large number of corporate cultures still hold the value that separation of people's business and personal lives is beneficial. Not only is this belief unrealistic, what it calls for is not possible. Over the years, you may have heard, or even voiced sentiments like, "Don't bring your personal problems to work." Or, conversely, at home, "Why don't you leave that business stuff at the office." No one but a certified schizophrenic knows how to do this. We are who we are and if we're having difficulties in our personal lives, they will surely reflect in our work product. Similarly, a tough time at work will impact on our personal lives.

Jack Kornfield, in his book *A Path With Heart*, (Bantam Books, 1993) deals with this tension succinctly. Mr. Kornfield writes, "This dualistic nature of thought is a root of our suffering. Whenever we think of ourselves as separate, fear and attachment arise and we grow constricted, defensive, ambitious, and territorial. To protect the separate self, we push certain things away, while to bolster it we hold on to other things and identify with them." This is the essence of "I am what I do."

What the suggestions here boil down to is a process of merging our lives into one greater whole rather than splitting it into discreet sections. Directly linking what we really want for ourselves with what our employer can reasonably provide is a point at which true buy-in can be achieved. Imagine what your business would be like if people routinely shared their personal plans and aspirations with their managers and colleagues and that, indeed, this sharing was honored as a significant part of the normal work environment. Suppose, for instance, that one of your key executive's personal plans is to leave the business in three years and relocate to another part of the country in order to be close to his or her family. Wouldn't it be nice to have that information right away instead of getting the traditional two-to-four week notice and having to scramble to cover the void left by such a departure?

When we seriously acknowledge the realities that people do not stay forever and that not everyone is motivated by the same things, we begin to view our business enterprises in a totally different light. Our job increasingly becomes developing the people and keeping them engaged by helping them achieve their goals and dreams and decreasingly to manage and control the business. After all, isn't building the business what we hired *them* to do? In our example, the company could actually partner with the departing executive to meet his or her needs for the next three years and do timely, open, succession planning to better manage the transition. Look, the executive is going to leave anyway. Wouldn't it be better to know and manage the transition rather than be surprised by an unforeseen resignation? The kind of openness of which we're speaking about here is rare in most organizations. Why? Because traditionally people have been judged disloyal for leaving companies and therefore they fear retribution for being honest about their life plans.

The same fear exists around quality-of-life issues. During a recent client engagement, I was working with the managing partner of an international accounting firm on their management development needs. In one meeting, he expressed frustration at, and disappointment with, one of his senior managers for not wanting to become a partner. This particular manager had a good, solid family life and was dedicated to a quality of life that allowed him ample time with his wife and children. Being a partner in this specific firm meant that he could have to work 60-plus hours a week and thus be away from home more that he was willing to do. During the meeting, I asked the managing partner if there were anything lacking in this particular senior manager's performance. The response was "no." In fact, this individual had exceeded his plan for the previous year and was on track to do the same in the current year. I then asked what the problem was. The answer, while predictable, is telling. The managing partner said that this individual was capable of doing much more and that, even though he was exceeding their agreed upon-plan, he hadn't worked very hard to do it, and his lack of interest in becoming a partner was proof of his lack of commitment to his career. At this firm, people who are serious about their careers *always* want to become partners.

Unfortunately, this model is alive and well in all too many organizations in America today. Because of the culture in this firm and his own beliefs about what having a career really means, this executive was setting up a dynamic that, if not altered, would cause a regular producer of good results and a loyal employee to leave. In the managing partner's world view, it simply was not possible for a bright, competent individual to remain at the senior manager level. That would set a bad example for others in the company!

Instead of viewing the senior manager as a problem that needed fixing, the managing partner could have seen the situation more positively. How? He could have realized that he had a good, steady producer on his hands that he could count on year after year. After all, the senior manager never indicated that he wanted to leave the firm. He never said that he was unwilling to learn new things and grow in his position. He simply was public about his unwillingness to work the kind of hours that it took to become a partner. He had other priorities in his life. His cardinal sin was being open about it. This situation could have been very different if the culture of the organization supported balance in their employees' lives and provided room for both people who wanted to work the long hours and those who didn't. Ultimately, the senior manager left the firm for another where the values were better aligned with his own.

It is in circumstances such as the one just described where the Personal Vision Statement can become an essential tool in working out business strategy. Remember, you want your team members to follow your lead and craft their individual visions. Once you have gotten buy-in and colleagues have actually gone through the same process that you have completed, you are ready to meet as a group and share your individual Personal Vision Statements.

This meeting should be held off-site for a full day. (The use of a facilitator is recommended as, initially, you may be dealing with some sensitive issues, and a professional facilitator can help guide the team around any psychological land mines.)

This type of meeting is a major undertaking for most management teams, but don't expect miracles just because you have arranged this meeting. What you can expect here is an increased level of communication and trust to develop among the team members. Many mature, healthy teams find that this experience actually is the beginning of a path that leads to an enhanced level of cooperation and performance. Newer teams find the experience to be a solid foundation on which to build in the future.

Remember: We are at the beginning of a long journey and must keep in context where we are and what we can reasonably expect. If the sharing of personal vision is treated as an event and not as part of an overall long-term process, what will likely be achieved is a short-term "feel good" but no long-term change.

With some of the personal and structural work underway and a better understanding of the changing roles of people in your organization, it is now time to focus on the next level of learning.

This learning is at the psychological level and is where the real leverage exists. For many organizations, dealing directly with behavioral issues has not been part of the culture. In fact, in some situations, you would be penalized for these kind of interventions. Human resource organizations in some companies have positioned themselves as the only acceptable resource to deal with "sensitive" issues, thus solidifying *their* position in the hierarchy. In still other organizations, failed attempts to introduce so-called leading edge programs dealing with the behavioral component have damaged many careers.

What I am suggesting is not a program but rather a shift in the cultural values of the organization. If we are to succeed, over the long run, so-called "sensitive" issues must be normalized and dealt with by employees at all levels as routine, daily work practice.

Let us be clear that certain issues are indeed "sensitive" and should be held in confidence and dealt with in privacy. However, poor work performance, repetitive errors, inappropriate behavior and the like need to be addressed by those closest to the work in a supportive environment that honors creative solutions and solid coaching. In other words, if a colleague is behaving in a manner not consistent with the values and/or mission of the organization, you get to say, "Knock it off" and they get to say, "Thanks for the heads up." I know this sounds oversimplified but, with practice, everyone in the organization can build skills in the areas of positive confrontation and problem solving.

For example, if a stated value of the organization is *no talking about your colleagues when they are not present* and you are involved in such a hallway conversation, a passing employee who overhears the conversation has the responsibility to point out the violation of the corporate values and not fear retribution for their courage. They get to say, "Hey, guys, we don't do that around here. Wouldn't it be better to get together with Fred and work *with* him on a solution to the problem?" Imagine an office worker saying that to a group of executives in most organizations. Now imagine the power of that kind of proactive coaching and courageous leadership in *your* company! This is the kind of environment we are talking about. These are the kind of skills we must develop.

CHAPTER SIX

Transforming Your Organization:

Now Your Work Group

It is time for the next big step in the process, an interesting one: the linking of the Personal Vision Statements to the organization. We have already identified the "What's In It For Me" aspect. Now, we establish what the organization can reasonable do to help meet some of the individual needs of their employees.

We do this by crafting a Work Group Mission Statement that embraces many of the individual team member's visions. By "Mission Statement," we are not talking about the one you probably already have hanging on your wall or printed in your brochure or annual report. We are talking, rather, about creating a document that is specific to your team and that addresses what the company and each individual will do to establish a true partnership for mutual benefit. In other words, a win-win work agreement.

From executive teams to teams on the shop floor, work groups are beginning to understand that, by working together cooperatively, everyone can get what they need and want easier and faster than by employing our more familiar adversarial model. Linking what we want with what our organizations can reasonably provide is the beginning of true empowerment based on personal responsibility and cooperation. Easy to say, not so easy to do, for we are talking about destroying barriers, both structural and belief-system based, that have existed for decades.

When we think about developing a Work Group Mission Statement, some of the following thoughts spring to mind:

* "We need to spend three or four hours talking about our mission and goals."
* "It's about time. Now maybe we can figure out where we are supposed to be going."
* Does it take *that* long to talk about our purpose?"
* "Oh no! Not that again! We've been there before."
* "I don't know what the problem is. I know exactly why we are here. Doesn't everyone else?"
* "They gotta be kidding! We've never gotten anywhere talking about that general stuff. Let's just get back to work."

From such popular comments it is safe to say that most people don't get overly excited about the prospect of developing a mission statement. Over the years, all of us have likely been exposed to this kind of process numerous times and, all too often, the effort has resulted in the creation of some general, lukewarm statement about "apple pie and motherhood." Once we have created our mission statement, it gets published in a variety of ways and then we go about our daily lives with little or no thought devoted to what the words mean. The primary reason for this behavior is that we have no real emotional attachment to the mission. The "What's In It For Me" is missing.

The Work Group Mission Statement we recommend here is vastly different in that it intentionally comprehends as much of the individual team member's Personal Vision Statements as is reasonably possible. What we want to do is to directly link what people want and need in their lives to what the employment situation can actually provide. When this linkage is accomplished, people begin to view coming to work in a very different way. When this link is forged, your work efforts are directly tied to your personal wants and needs. You (not the company) are responsible for achieving the things in your life that are important to you. You begin to see that your daily efforts translate into concrete accomplishments that improve the quality of life, as you have defined it, for you and your family. Career decisions can now be tested against the criteria articulated in your Personal Vision Statement and your Work Group Mission Statement. In effect, you have formed a basic work contract. You will do certain things for yourself, the organization, and the team—and the organization will do certain things for you and the team. A win-win work agreement.

In terms of process, each team member should write their own Work Group Mission Statement in a way that they feel expresses their needs, while comprehending the overall mission of the organization and their specific work team. As with the Personal Vision Statement, this procedure, too, should be performed by the top management team first to serve as a model for virtually all work teams in the organization.

Once all of the team members have their first cut, the team should meet in a series of facilitated meetings to combine the various statements into a single statement that has unanimous agreement. What you want to come out with is a single Work Group Mission Statement that defines what the team does and the value it adds to the organization, as well as what each team member will get as it relates to their Personal Vision Statement.

This process is mostly a hard one; hence, the recommendation for a series of meetings. Experience has proven that attempting to do this in a "one shot" off-site is not effective. People need more time to consider the needs of the team and their fellow team members. It is no easy task to talk about what we actually want and then to fashion our work to provide those things. People may find that some of the individual needs appear to be in conflict with others and that some negotiation is required in order to reach agreement.

In this negotiation phase, take care not to move to compromise early just to complete the task. What you want to do is practice the blending of personal hopes and dreams with your employment or business situation in a way that causes you to learn new skills and to normalize the process as just another part of being in business.

When I caution not to compromise early, what I really mean is not to compromise at all. Compromise unfortunately has all of the ear-marks of a lose-lose situation. In most compromises, what usually happens is that all the parties involved "give up" on something so that an agreement can be reached, thus sending everyone away with the feeling of getting less than what they wanted. What you are looking for here is the situation where everyone gets some, if not all of what they want. Our traditional model for negotiations is based on win-lose and a belief in scarcity. There is only so much money, power, recognition, position, etc. If you approach a negotiation from a belief in scarcity, in order for you to win, someone else must lose. (Or, if I get what I want, you will have to give up something or vice versa) This approach causes polarization and conflict. We should strive to arrange for everyone to get enough of what they want so that they come away from the negotiation with a feeling of satisfaction.

True win-win negotiations can be created when the parties involved come to the table with a different belief system in place; that is, the belief in abundance. If you can believe that there is more than enough money, power, recognition and the like for everyone to have what they want, then you are free to create situations where that is possible. Giving up a belief in scarcity and embracing one of abundance can do more to create wealth in all aspects of your life than anything else you can do. If you limit yourself by your own thinking, you are doomed to repeat the same old patterns. On the other hand, if you learn to think outside the box, you can create whatever it is that you want.

Be thoughtful and prudent about these negotiations, don't rush the process. Your meetings can be held in the work place or off-site. Don't make them marathons, a couple of hours at a time is plenty. Have fun with the process. Learn about your colleagues and yourself, and apply that learning to all other facets of your life.

Now, let's see where we are. So far, each member of the team has created a Personal Vision Statement and the team has met to share the content of those visions with each other. After learning about each other's values, goals, and plans, the team has crafted a

Work Group Mission Statement through meeting over a period of, say, several months. You now have identified what each team member wants and have articulated how the organization can meet some or all of those needs.

The next phase of our journey deals with the organization's system of rewards and recognition. All too often, systems, processes, and programs are introduced into organizations when halfway through their implementation it is discovered that the compensation systems are not aligned with the behavior that the newly implemented programs are designed to encourage.

A classic example comes from a recent client of mine, a 100-year-old company in a high tech industry with revenues of several billion dollars per year. This company has long been run in a hierarchical manner and has developed what is commonly known in the business as "smoke stacks" or "silos," meaning that discreet functions in the firm have their own structure and hierarchy that routinely do not communicate effectively with each other.

Due to severe market conditions combined with a bloated management structure and an absolute inability to respond to their customers in a timely manner, a new CEO was brought in a few years ago to change the culture and put the company back on track. During his first year, the CEO went on the road and visited approximately 400 customers, face to face. Upon his return, he announced a major reorganization that would eliminate seven layers of management existing between him and the customers. In addition to this major downsizing, he began implementing self-managed work teams that would concentrate on all of their major customers and customer opportunities. Consultants were brought in to help with the transition. Extensive training was done on the new model and people were laid off, transferred, or reassigned. During the first three years, significant resources were put into managing the transition from this traditional, top-down structure into the flatter, self-managed, more responsive model. Empowerment was the order of the day. Personal responsibility, virtual organizational structures, coaches, and associates were all part of the new language of their culture.

It all sounds pretty good and indeed much of what they did was right on point. However, they missed some critical elements in the change process that caused the transition to be more painful and costly than it needed to be.

First of all, the organization had always had a strong sales bias. Selling the equipment that they manufactured was all that was truly honored in their culture. Support, software, and other professional services were seen as necessary but unimportant, and were frequently used as bargaining chips in negotiations with customers. Awards and recognition were handed out to sales executives and sales people routinely. A special parking space was reserved for the "salesman of the month" at most offices, and the major management positions and plum assignments usually went to people in the sales organization. As expected, a fair amount of animosity festered in various other parts of the organization, and the resulting resentment had become part of the fabric of the corporation.

When the reorganization information came down from on high, many of the people responsible for the reassigning of the existing staff were actually the same people who had been running the business for many years—the sales people. Not surprisingly, they assigned former sales managers and executives to the new positions as team leaders, accomplishing little more than transplanting the old culture into the new organizational model. People throughout the organization recognized these moves for what they were, a reshuffling of people with no real change in business practice and behavior. Managers did some version of, "They may have changed the structure, but I'm still in charge and sales still makes the decisions around here." You can well imagine the reaction of people throughout the company to this newly espoused philosophy when the behavior was business as usual. Opportunity for new leadership was missed.

One vital factor missed was the alignment of the rewards and recognition systems with the new organizational model.

Historically, compensation of the sales force was based on gross sales of the equipment they sold. Although there were guidelines regarding profit margins, compensation depended solely on gross sales. Software and professional services were considered giveaways. Generally, the sales people did not pay that much attention to these portions of the business.

Along with the new organizational model, the company announced that the sale of software and services were it's new future and that the dependence on equipment sales had to be changed. The CEO charged Human Resources with the job of formulating a new compensation model for the sales and professional services people that would drive the new behaviors required under the new rules. Along with the bias toward equipment sales, the company also had a widely held belief system within the professional services ranks that they were there to "help" the customers and they shouldn't have to sell their services. Statements such as these were heard throughout the company: "I didn't take this job to be a salesman"; "I've never had to sell anything to *my* customers before and I'm not about to start now"; and, "My customers won't trust me to do the right thing for them if I have to sell myself to them."

What actually happened in implementation was that Human Resources ran into roadblock after roadblock from the sales organization in their attempt to change the compensation model, and management throughout the company felt the resistance of the professional services staff.

Three years later, they had a sales compensation system that had begun to address the new organizational model. That year, 10 percent of the salesperson's business had to come from selling professional services, (leaving 90 percent still coming from equipment sales) and, on the teams, if they didn't make their goals for the year, there would be some impact on the salesperson's income. Hardly a bold stroke. Meanwhile, you still had the company's management and the consultants espousing the new philosophy.

This situation is a crazy maker! Crazy as defined by continuing to do the same things and expecting different results. People continue to work in self-managed work teams led by individuals that largely know only special privilege and hierarchical management techniques. The company's published strategy is to aggressively grow their software and professional services business, but they continue to support a compensation model that drives behaviors contrary to the strategy. Reorganizations and downsizing continues, keeping people in a constant state of fear for their jobs while working 60 to 80 hours a week in a structure that doesn't make any sense to them.

How could much of this contradiction been avoided? First by recognizing that most people are not willing or able to dramatically alter their behaviors on their own. The new CEO made critical assumptions that proved problematic. He assumed, for example, that because *he* knew that these things were the right things to do and that *he* had asked for them to be done, that they would be. Then, he didn't assign absolute drop dead dates for completing these major changes. Finally, he trusted that this mandate would occur without having an appropriate follow-up and monitoring system in place.

These are common mistakes that executives make when they are downright convinced that they are doing the right things for the business. But people do not always act in their own best interest, even though it may seem obvious to some that it makes sense to do so. Attitudes, belief systems and biases are not always rational, and just because something makes sense doesn't mean it will be done. People routinely act in ways that not only counter their best interest but that are, from time to time, self-destructive. What is obvious to one person may seem to be totally ludicrous to another.

Also, when major change initiatives follow a corporate downsizing, the people remaining are in various stages of shock. They are in the process of mourning for those laid off, they are dealing with their own guilt as survivors ("Why didn't I get the axe too?"), and they are fearful that they might be next. Careful attention to these signs of unmanaged transition can prevent disaster. Just telling people to "get on with it" is usually not sufficient—you must have the skills to help people get through the tough times and understand how to facilitate individuals and groups through the transition.

Addressing the growing problem of aligning rewards and recognition systems to foster the behaviors required to support a new model, we present a brief checklist that will help guide you through the process.

CHECKLIST FOR ALIGNMENT OF REWARDS AND RECOGNITION SYSTEMS

1. Insure that all functions and work groups have a current Work Group Mission Statement.
2. Insure that all functions and work groups have clearly articulated and measurable performance goals and objectives.
3. Survey employees to determine what type of incentive programs they would like to see implemented.
4. Determine formulas for base wage and salary rates as well as performance incentive bonuses. Insure that these align with the stated mission of the organization.
5. Avoid "one size fits all" rewards and recognition programs. Tailor the systems to meet as many different situations as possible.
6. Insure that employer contributions to any program that is in addition to base wage, salary, and/or commission structure is determined by financial performance of the overall organization.
7. Institute regular recognition programs to recognize work groups and individuals who routinely contribute to the success of the organization.
8. Avoid selective recognition and rewards systems. For example, sales and marketing have top performer clubs/awards, but other functions in the organization do not.
9. Create systems that are based on both individual and work group success.
10. Don't expect money to cure all ills. Find out what works for today and be willing to change it tomorrow when it is no longer effective.

As you work through the process of transforming your organization, it is vitally important to pay attention to the timing and sequence of events. The rewards and recognition system component of any organization is key to supporting the specific behaviors that are required in order to operate within a given model.

As we have discussed, in our traditional hierarchical structures, the required behavior for managers was to do the thinking, planning, and other analytical work and then to issue directives to the workers about what to do, how to do it, and when to have it done. Management was then to check up on the workers in order to control the process and insure that things got done. In this same structure, workers were to respond with compliance, to do the work, and to not question management's motives or methods. In short, managers were compensated for being in charge and for insuring that the work got done through compliance of the workers. Workers were compensated for showing up, keeping their mouths shut, and following the rules.

In a flatter, team-based organization, all employees need to be compensated for using their skill, creativity, innovativeness, and guts. People need to be encouraged to challenge traditional thinking, not punished for it. Skills and behaviors once strictly the territory of management are now required for all employees. These major behavioral changes do not occur quickly. It is crucial that we do not make the transition even more difficult by saying one thing and doing another.

When you are transforming an organization from one particular culture and structure to another, you must be prepared for the barriers and pitfalls of the new model and have a well-crafted plan to accomplish the transformation over a number of years. Preparing your rewards and recognition systems well in advance of any major organizational change will help to smooth the transition. Remember what these systems do for us is drive specific behaviors. If you pay me ten dollars to do "A" and one dollar to do "B," I'll do "A" every time, regardless of what you may be telling me to the contrary.

An essential next step in your organizational transformation is the institutionalization of a true 360-degree feedback process, which has many different interpretations. For the purpose of this writing, the 360-degree feedback is defined as a normal business process whereby employees at all levels solicit and receive regular feedback from their colleagues on how they and their function are performing. In a true 360-degree system, there are no sacred cows; everything is on the table.

Employees are invited to confront their managers about their ideas, methods, and behaviors without fear of retribution. Likewise, managers are expected to confront their direct reports and fellow managers around the same issues. In an organization where this process is perceived as an integral part of the culture (and therefore company success), this feedback process crosses all lines of function and level.

Let us be cautious about our definition of confrontation and the methods that we employ using it. Confrontation does not mean "getting in someone's face" every time something doesn't go the way we would like. What it does mean is that we should be free to exchange thoughts, ideas, and opinions openly and without judgment.

The 360-degree feedback process can take on any number of shapes. I always like to deal with the practical realities in any client engagement when instituting this process. First of all, you must establish the levels of trust and openness that are currently present in your organization. It is equally important to examine both organizational reality and myths. For example, I have heard it said again and again by people in organizations that they can't do X because "they will get in trouble if they do." In the great majority of the cases, when I ask, "When was the last time someone in this organization got fired, disciplined, or otherwise sanctioned for doing X?" The answer is "almost never." This reality does not, however, seem to effect the belief system that persists.

Logic does not always drive people; in fact, when emotion is involved, logic seldom prevails. Therefore, when examining ourselves and our organizations, we must be sensitive to both "our" truths and "the" truths that exist. Where we get ourselves into trouble is when "our truth" becomes "the truth."

In organizations where this kind of open, honest feedback is not currently part of the culture, you may want to begin with an anonymous survey (providing a safe environment) to establish what people think of your organization's culture. These surveys have value in that they usually ask some very good questions however they can, and are often used as an outlet for people to vent their anger and frustration. Don't let this discourage you from continuing the process because some excellent data is also contained in the same survey. The most important part of any survey is to provide feedback to the participants as to what the findings were and what will be done to address the specific issues identified. If you are unwilling to do something about the issues, don't bother with the survey. Remember, just surveying people sets up a level of expectation that something will be done with the findings and that something will change.

Many organizations have been doing surveys for years with varied results. Some have even abandoned the practice because they have not been able to track any tangible results from their efforts. There can be a myriad of reasons for this inability. It could be due to the organization's unwillingness or incapability to deal with what it discovered. Or it could be that the time between the survey and change was so great (with no feedback in between) that the people felt as if they had not been heard.

In organizations where the level of trust is higher, written surveys in which the respondents are identified by name and function are an even better tool. By knowing who said what, you know to whom to address specific feedback and who to go to for more information. This level of open, honest data exchange can lay the groundwork for an environment of true 360-degree feedback. As you read and use the survey information and provide feedback to the respondents, you have an opportunity to discover important facts about your businesses as well as build the open environment that will allow you to become the flexible, dynamic enterprise that you must.

Finally, true 360-degree feedback exists when all employees can approach each other with issues of business process, ethics, style, finance, and any other subject with the reasonable expectation that they will be heard and considered. Now, not every suggestion or idea is a pearl; some are real klinkers. That is not the point. What counts is that all ideas and thoughts and opinions are considered, and the effort in bringing them to the table is honored and rewarded. If only one percent of new ideas turn into profitable changes for your business, you are far ahead of where you would have been without those ideas.

As you establish this culture of open sharing of ideas and thoughts, you will find that the level and quality of the communication, teamwork, and actual ideas increases the more you practice. Like any other skill, don't expect perfection the first time out. Perfection is not what you're after here, cultural and behavioral change is.

To get you started, a sample survey is presented.

COMPANY NAME

MANAGEMENT SURVEY

NAME: _____

The purpose of this questionnaire is to provide each member of management with feedback on his or her job performance from a somewhat different viewpoint; that is, from the viewpoint of the people reporting directly to the manager. You are requested to assess your manager in terms of his or her effectiveness in communicating, coaching, encouraging participative management, and leadership techniques.

For each statement select the number that best represents your opinion of your supervisor's effectiveness. If, for any reason, you are unable to rate the person on a particular item, leave it blank.

5 = Strongly agree
4 = Agree
3 = Neither agree nor disagree
2 = Disagree
1 = Strongly disagree

Take your time and give your answers some thought. Be as honest as possible. Below each area there is room for any comments you would like to make regarding the person's effectiveness in that area.

COMMUNICATION/PARTICIPATIVE MANAGEMENT

1. _____Guidelines, concerns, and decisions are provided in a clear and timely manner that better enables me to do my job.

2. _____He/she listens attentively and insures he/she understands what I am saying.

3. _____He/she answers my questions clearly and completely.

4. _____He/she provides me with sufficient information to enable me to perform my job.

5. _____My opinion and thinking is solicited on matters pertaining to my areas of responsibility.

6. _____He/she encourages me to express my opinion even if not in agreement with it.

7. _____He/she communicates the reasons for decisions that effect my area of responsibility.

8. _____He/she encourages me to be innovative in accomplishing my work.

Additional comments: _____
_____
_____
_____

COACHING/PROVIDING FEEDBACK

9. _____My manager provides me with specific and constructive feedback about my performance. I know where I stand.

10. _____My manager has negotiated my department's goals for this year with me.

11. _____My manager insures that there is complete and correct information before rating any direct report's performance.

12. _____He/she acknowledges a job well done.

Additional comments: _____

_____

_____

_____

_____

LEADERSHIP TECHNIQUES

13. _____He/she sets an example and role model by personal actions and management style that motivates me.

14. _____He/she provides me with the appropriate amount of direction and guidance in the accomplishment of my work.

15. _____He/she implements and acts upon suggestions for improvement as soon as possible.

16. _____He/she takes actions necessary to remove roadblocks that prevent me from accomplishing my goals.

17. _____He/she provides a supportive environment in which mistakes can be made and learned from.

18. _____He/she encourages teamwork within my group.

Additional comments: _____

_____

_____

_____

_____

PLEASE COMPLETE THE
FOLLOWING SENTENCES

A. The things I would like my manager to do *more* of are:

    1. _____

    2. _____

    3. _____

B. The things I would like my manager to do *less* of are:

    1. _____

    2. _____

    3. _____

C. The things I would like my manager to do the *same* of are:

    1. _____

    2. _____

    3. _____

Additional comments: _____

_____

_____

_____

NAME: _____

MANAGEMENT SURVEY

DIRECT REPORTS (8)

Sample Rating System Scores

	1	2	3	4	5	Avg.
1. Guidelines, concerns and decisions are provided in a clear and timely manner that better enables me to do my job.		1	5	2		2.63
2. He/she listens attentively and understands what I am saying.	2	1	2	2	1	2.88
3. He/she answers my questions clearly and completely.	1	2		4	1	3.25
4. He/she provides me with sufficient information to enable me to perform my job.	1	3		4		2.88
5. My opinion is solicited on matters pertaining to my area of responsibility.	1	1	2	2	2	3.38
6. He/she encourages me to express my opinion even if not in agreement with it.		1	2	4	1	3.63
7. He/she communicates the reasons for decisions made that effect my area of responsibility.	1		4	2	1	3.25
8. He/she encourages me to be innovative in accomplishing my work.			2	4	2	4.00

COACHING/PROVIDING FEEDBACK

	1	2	3	4	5	Avg.
9. My manager provides me with specific and constructive feedback about my performance. I know where I stand.	1	2	2	2	1	3.00
10. My manager has negotiated my department's goals with me for this year.	2	2		3	1	2.88
11. My manager insures that there is complete and correct information before rating my performance.	1	1	4		1	2.71
12. He/she acknowledges a job well done.		2		4	2	3.75

LEADERSHIP TECHNIQUES

	1	2	3	4	5	Avg.
13. He/she sets an example and role model by personal actions and management style that motivates me.	2	3		2	1	2.63
14. He/she provides me with the appropriate amount of guidance in the accomplishment of my work.	1	3	1	2	1	2.88
15. He/she implements and acts upon suggestions for improvement as soon as possible.		2	1	4	1	3.5
16. He/she takes actions necessary to remove roadblocks that prevent me from accomplishing my goals.	1		3	3	1	3.38
17. He/she provides a supportive environment in which mistakes can be made and learned from.	1	1	3	2	1	3.13
18. He/she encourages teamwork within my group.		1	2	2	2	3.71

SUMMARY COMMENT: _____

_____

_____

_____

Having established the linkage between personal vision and work group mission for you and your team, and creating a repeatable 360-degree feedback process, you are well on your way towards transforming your organization.

By now you and your team should have experienced powerful results from working together in these new and different ways. The benefits will be obvious and you are likely anxious to spread these processes throughout your organization.

If you have been "selling" the process at every step, you should not have too much trouble. On the other hand, if you have been operating in relatively secrecy, waiting to see how it works before letting others know what you are up to, you may find people far more resistant to getting started themselves. Remember, you must be committed and enthusiastic throughout the process. If you are not, others will be far less likely to follow your lead.

In Chapter Seven, we provide you with more of the road map for transformation and additional tools and resources to aid you in your journey.

CHAPTER SEVEN

Transforming Your Organization:
The Entire Enterprise

In previous chapters, we have talked about history, background, certain processes and tools as pieces of the complex puzzle of organizational transformation. Now it is time to summarize what we have done and pull it all together in a comprehensive, chronologically oriented approach to the process. As you are now aware, there is no one formula for organizational transformation, but there are certain steps you can take that have proven to be common in any transformation process. Let's examine these in the sequence they most often occur. I'll comment on each step regarding things to do and things not to do based on my accumulative experience.

Please do not take these steps as a concrete approach to your organizational transformation. Remember, each situation is different and every organization approaches the process from a slightly different perspective based upon its history, people, and current business situation. At every step, people learn new insights concerning themselves and their organizational situation and adapt the process to match their needs. An overly structured, "one size fits all" approach to this work is inappropriate and will not generate the kind of results you are striving for.

Organizational transformation takes place slowly, over time, like the aging of a fine wine. While boldness is advisable in some phases, caution must be exercised in others. It is more an art than a science. Each phase of the transformation must be measured, evaluated, and critiqued for the desired results. Since you are dealing with both the structural and human behavioral components in practical application, you must be critical of both the process and the outcome, with particular emphasis on the process. When I say critical, I do not mean it in a negative way, but rather in its evaluative form. You must constantly evaluate what you are doing and how you are doing it, with an eye towards improving both the outcome obtained and the process by which you achieved it.

Some of the most common questions I get from clients when discussing this type of work are, "What is the desired result we should be looking for from doing all this work?" and, "How are we to be sure that we are doing it the right way?" To both of these and many others, I usually respond with questions of my own. Responding to a question about results, I will usually ask clients what results they want to achieve. After all, it's *their* business, not mine. As I have said, we are a culture of rule followers and are constantly seeking the "right" way to do most things. In my experience, there are a wide variety of "right" ways to accomplish the transformation of an organization. It is more important to get started than to continually search for the one "right" way.

If you are in a business situation where you are routinely achieving your organizational, cultural, and financial goals, you probably do not need to undertake an aggressive transformation process. Although few and far between, organizations do exist where major work has already been done and, consequently, only continued fine tuning is required. On the other hand, if your organization exhibits some of the characteristics we have discussed, if productivity is not where you want it, morale is not at a level that supports high-performance individuals and teams, or you just seem to be working more and enjoying it less, you may be ready to begin the journey.

We began by following the guidelines in Chapters Five and Six: Personal Vision Statements have been created by members of the executive team and quite possibly by many other management and non-management employees. These visions have been shared in the work group environment, and Mission Statements have been crafted that comprehend elements of each member's vision. You have established an atmosphere of open and honest coaching by practicing 360-degree feedback and have begun to create a continuous learning environment.

The next step is one of further exploration. You must broaden your efforts and find out what others in your organization think about the business, their position in it, and their ability and willingness to champion change. Begin this process with a series of formal and informal discussions with your team and others throughout the organization. You need to gain a "feel" for the culture and how people operate in it. This is often a difficult task for senior management because people frequently tell you what they think you want to hear rather than what they really think and feel. Don't be frustrated by initial attempts at gathering this information. Give it time, and remember to be abundantly clear about why you are going around asking all these strange questions. People must know that you have something specific in mind and that you are interested in a long-term transformation of the corporate culture. In this initial phase, remember all of the built-in biases against much of what you are attempting to do and use the knowledge and tools you have acquired to help people over the hurdles of their own attitudes, belief systems, and biases.

Once you have laid the groundwork for your data gathering, it is frequently useful to conduct an organizational health survey as a means to gather formal data on how your employees perceive the organization. As you are no doubt aware, surveys are nothing new and you have likely conducted them in your organization in the past, possibly recently. If you have current data, you may wish to proceed to more aggressive and personal methods, such as dialog groups. If you have not surveyed your employees recently, this can be an important step in building the trust required for effective organizational transformation.

Internal surveys can be a double-edged sword in that they gather data on the subject at hand, which is what you want, but they also create expectations in the minds of those surveyed that something is actually going to be done with that data collected, which is something you may or may not want. The short course is:

If you really don't want to know, don't ask. Many organizations have created false expectations in employees by conducting surveys only to do nothing with the information collected, further frustrating their people. In even more damaging situations, no feedback at all has been provided to those surveyed, reinforcing the belief that management only does these kind of things because they think they should, but they really do not care what their people think.

We include here a typical Organizational Health Survey (p. 126) to serve as a model for use in your organization. As with any survey, this one should be customized to meet the particular needs of your organization and the target audience.

SAMPLE SURVEY

(Circle the descriptor that best represents your
opinion of the following issues)

1. Employees are continually setting and achieving short and long-term financial, operational and personal development goals.

   Poor   Fair   Good   Very   Good   Excellent

   Comments: _____
   _____
   _____
   _____

2. Employees work as a team, but accept individual accountability for their assignments.

   Poor   Fair   Good   Very   Good   Excellent

   Comments: _____
   _____
   _____
   _____

3. Employees have and willingly share the essential information needed for all of us to do our work.

   Poor   Fair   Good   Very   Good   Excellent

   Comments: _____
   _____
   _____
   _____

4. Employees understand their roles within their group and they have the freedom and responsibility to continuously improve the process and systems necessary to perform their work.

Poor   Fair   Good   Very   Good   Excellent

Comments: _____

_____

_____

_____

_____

5. Employees understand the roles of their group and believe the group has the freedom and responsibility to continuously improve the processes and systems necessary for the group to perform its work.

Poor   Fair   Good   Very   Good   Excellent

Comments: _____

_____

_____

_____

6. Employees continually increase their capabilities to perform their jobs and they take responsibility to prepare themselves for additional opportunities as their interests and capabilities match company needs.

Poor   Fair   Good   Very   Good   Excellent

Comments: _____

_____

_____

_____

7. Employees are fairly compensated and recognized for the value
    they contribute to the company.

    Poor   Fair   Good   Very   Good   Excellent

Comments: _____
_____
_____
_____

8. General respect and cooperation shown between managers and
    their staff.

    Poor   Fair   Good   Very   Good   Excellent

Comments: _____
_____
_____
_____
_____

9. Overall staffing levels in the company.

    Poor   Fair   Good   Very   Good   Excellent

Comments: _____
_____
_____
_____

10. Overall teamwork in the company.

    Poor   Fair   Good   Very   Good   Excellent

Comments: _____
_____
_____
_____

11. Overall consistency of the organization in management approach, policy formulation, and implementation.

Poor   Fair   Good   Very   Good   Excellent

Comments: _____

_____

_____

_____

12. Overall progress in improving organizational health in the last 2 years.

Poor   Fair   Good   Very   Good   Excellent

Comments: _____

_____

_____

_____

13. General Comments: _____

_____

_____

_____

_____

_____

Surveys can be conducted throughout the organization to gather general information (as in the previous example) or can be targeted at certain areas within the organization to gather "work specific" information. If you desire a quantitative result from which to work, simply assign a numerical value to the rating. For example: Poor = 1, Fair =2, Good = 3, Very good = 4, Excellent = 5.

You may choose to survey on an anonymous basis initially and move to a known respondent version when you feel you will receive candid responses from your employees. If there is a lack of trust in the organization or a history (or perceived history) of retribution for speaking up on issues, you obviously will not get the true information you are seeking.

Once you have a good feel for the culture and belief systems within your organization, you may want to employ a more advanced technique for gathering this type of information as well as creating an environment and a forum for organizational transformation. Dialog groups are one of these techniques. Dialog groups are formed to surface the deeper belief systems of individuals and groups within organizations and are usually chartered in an open ended fashion. By open ended, I mean that they have no specific outcome in mind other than exploration, and that they may exist for months and even years.

David Bohm, a leading contemporary physicist and strong proponent of dialog in science, business, and community has described the phenomenon of dialog as occurring "when a group becomes open to the flow of a larger intelligence." Dialog, as practiced by the ancient Greeks and many other early societies, such as the American Indians, was a means to discover "the truth" by creating something that was greater than the sum of the individual parts. Dialog groups have described their experiences as the process "taking on a life of it's own." This leverage is one of the crucial elements in organizational transformation. Learning "the truth" about your organization and it's culture and creating vehicles for change are essential to beginning a successful transformation process.

Remember, dialog comes from the Greek *dialogos*. Dia means through. *Logos* means "the word" or "the meaning." Bohm has suggested the original meaning of dialog was "meaning passing or moving through. A free flow of meaning between people." In a dialog group, there are no winners or losers. It is not a contest to see who can come up with the best ideas or how fast a particular problem can be solved. Dialog groups exist to create understanding and leverage in the organization. An understanding and practice of systems thinking and team learning are essential to a successful dialog group. The ability to "suspend assumptions" is the cornerstone of any successful dialog group. In addition, participants must relate to each other as colleagues, and a facilitator must keep the dialog in context.

A dialog group chartered to deal with the issues of organizational and cultural transformation must be free to create the structure and culture that the collective group wishes to. The facilitator must insure people do not get trapped by their own thinking. For example, statements such as, "They will never let us do that" or, "That isn't possible in this business" are examples of assumptions not suspended. The facilitator is responsible, in part, for moving individuals and the group away from these thought processes and into more creative realms where more is possible.

In a recent client meeting at a major medical center, one of the senior staff responded to my inquiry about physician behavior with a categorical statement declaring, "we'll never get the doctors to do that." This was a classic example of an assumption not suspended and was a genuine opportunity for the group to polarize around such a definitive statement. Instead of behaving in that way, we continued down our path of inquiry and asked for more information on why she believed this so strongly. She proceeded with much of the history already known by the group and in the process of doing so discovered that she was stuck in an old mental model about how doctors behave. In addition, she discovered that because she was also a physician, she was having trouble seeing herself behaving in these new and different ways, and was projecting that image onto the affiliate physicians as a group.

With a minimal amount of time spent and some careful facilitation, we were able to get her to suspend that particular assumption for the remainder of the meeting, which allowed her to create a new possibility in her mind as well as removing her as a road block to progress in the meeting. Now, was she 100 percent transformed by the experience, and did she instantaneously adopt the new way of thinking? Of course not. What did occur was an opportunity for her to practice her skill of suspending assumptions with the help of the group, and it opened a door to expanded thinking for her.

To form a dialog group in your organization, first decide what the purpose of the group is to be. If your purpose it to address short-term operational issues, another format may be more appropriate. If you are interested in surfacing the realities of the culture in your organization, a dialog group can be a very valuable step. Keep the group size to less than ten members to gain maximum interaction and build group trust and openness.

At first it may be difficult for a group of individuals accustomed to rapid fire problem solving and task-oriented work to adapt to a format that is more long range in its thinking. People can become frustrated by their feelings of time wasted or the lack of structure. Structure certainly has its place, and many meetings require structure and specific pacing to accomplish their desired outcomes. Dialog groups are different. They are intended to surface deeply held feelings and to deal with organizational problems in a more systematic fashion rather than the symptomatic, quick fix methods we all know so well.

It is helpful during the first year of a group to keep the membership in tact. As groups mature, they move through a number of phases and various leadership roles are assumed by certain members. Whenever a permanent member of a group leaves or a new member is introduced, the group must totally reform itself by returning to phase one and redefining the various roles. If the membership is constantly changing, the group never truly forms and grows. Therefore, it is difficult, if not impossible, for them to produce any meaningful work. Individuals skilled in group dynamics can recognize these phases of development and leadership roles and can facilitate the group's growth process, but the various steps cannot be skipped.

As your dialog group develops, you will be able to see the trust and openness grow, assuming there are rules for behavior in the group and the facilitator is skilled in helping the group work within those rules. In organizational transformation work, it is helpful to have a mixture of functions and positions represented. A group comprised only of senior management or heavily stacked in that direction may not yield the results you are looking for. How will you specifically identify your cultural and belief system issues if the only perspective you are getting is from one strata of the organization? Obviously you will not, so be willing to mix it up. Ensure that line and staff, hourly and salaried, and management and non-management positions are represented. In this forum, your natural champions will shine. This is where people for whom openness and candor are second nature, and who are motivated to build a great organization, will excel.

As in any endeavor, value is determined by what you do with the knowledge gained from the experience. Knowledge not applied has little value and is normally lost over time. Knowledge applied can begin and sustain the organizational transformation process.

As you discover the true nature of your organizational culture, it is important that people develop new skills to deal with the changes that you choose to make. This is where many of the tools covered in Part Two of this book can be applied. Utilizing the various psychological instruments and tools to build the human behavior knowledge base of all employees is essential. As we keep emphasizing, managers and individual contributors alike need to develop new skills that will enable them to participate in the transformation process as well as be prepared to operate efficiently in the new organization as it emerges. It is in this new work of discovering the true culture of your organization, as well as in the day-to-day operations of your business, that you can effectively utilize the tools that are available.

In terms of other useful tools, there exists many valuable psychological instruments that allow you to assess and predict certain behaviors, modify work environments for maximum efficiency, screen employee candidates, and build trust and rapport among team members.

In the area of affective measurement tools, some of the more common instruments include the Myers-Briggs Type Indicator, which is available from:

Consulting Psychologists Press
577 College Avenue
Palo Alto, Ca. 94306
Phone: 415/969-8901

Myers-Briggs categorizes people in terms of four specific types of behaviors and provides information on how to deal with the different "types" of people. The instrument categorizes people in the areas of introversion or extraversion, sensation or intuition, thinking or feeling, and perceiving or judging. Using this instrument can provide you with a better understanding of some of your own behaviors, as well as those of the people around you.

Another good resource that deals with the Meyers-Briggs is the book *Please Understand Me: Character & Temperament Types* (David Keirsey and Marilyn Bates, Prometheus Nemesis Books, 1978.) In this work, the authors categorize the four types as Dionysian, Epimethean, Promethean, and Apollonian. Dianysians represent approximately 38 percent of the population and have a fundamental need to be free. They will not be tied down and they avoid many obligations. This personality type tends to live for the moment and avoids planning for the future. Epimetheans, like the Dianysians, also comprise approximately 38 percent of the population and have a great need to belong to and to be useful within, their respective societal units. Promethians, on the other hand, represent approximately 12 percent of the population and tend to have a strong need for power and control, while Apollonians, representing the other 12 percent, are the intuitive, feeling members of society.

These brief descriptions of psychological tools are not intended to provide you with great insight into any one particular instrument, but rather to give you a sense of the style and approach each exhibits to aid you in selecting one or more for use in your business.

Yet a different type dealing with human behavior is the Style Analysis, sometimes referred to as the DISC, which is based on William Marston's book, *Emotions of Normal People*. This instrument is mostly narrative in form and provides individuals and their colleagues with information on things such as their general characteristics, value to the organization, keys to managing, motivated style, and keys to motivating. Additionally, it provides you with your ideal work environment, with do's and dont's of communicating, tips for you on communicating with various differing personalities, and an action planning section in areas for improvement. The instrument is available in an Employee/Manager version, a Team Building version, a Sales version, and several others. The Style Analysis is available from

TTI Performance Systems, Ltd.
16020 North 77th Street
Scottsdale, Arizona 85260
Phone: 480/443-1077

Another analytical instrument is the Preview Assessment. Like the Style Analysis, the Preview Assessment is available in a number of formats and can be used as an individual assessment, manager/employee coaching, or pre-employment screening tool. The Preview Assessment measures people in several areas of ability, such as Numerical Reasoning, Motivation/Interests, and Personality. Again like the Style Analysis, this instrument scores individuals against a statistical data base and has the ability to compare others in the same job function thus allowing the organization to develop success profiles for specific job functions. Sten graphs are developed in each of the rated areas and compared to the data base and/or fellow employees in the same job function. The Preview Assessment is available from:

Preview Assessments International, Inc.
4525 Lake Shore Drive
Waco, Tx. 76710
Phone: 817/751-1644

A different type of instrument is the Kolbe Conative Index, or KCI. While most, if not all of the commonly used instruments measure either the cognitive (IQ) portion or the affective (feeling) portion of the brain, Kolbe measures the conative portion, or what we will actually do in given situations. Conation is your natural drive or volition. While the other instruments listed are valuable for what they measure (ability, tendencies, learned behaviors), the KCI measures what your natural makeup mandates you to do.

The KCI provides you with feedback in four specific areas: Fact Finder, Follow Thru, Quick Start, and Implementor. Fact finder measures your natural instinct and willingness to probe, research, data gather, and judge. People who score high in Fact Finder are usually pragmatic and realistic and have a high need for facts and data prior to making decisions.

Follow Thru measures your tendencies to plan, design, program and systematize things. People who score high in Follow Thru are theorists and pattern makers. These people are organized and comfortable with repeatable processes. They like to depend on routine for things they must do that they deem unimportant. They do not like to reinvent the wheel all the time. Follow Thru, in this case, does not mean follow-up or detail work.

Quick Start measures your willingness to innovate, promote, and act as a catalyst for action. Quick Starts are entrepreneurs and people who get things going. They frequently require little data before making decisions.

Finally, Implementor measures your willingness to manufacture, mold, build, handcraft or handle specific things or tasks. Implementors are detail-oriented people. They are the people who will get things done. They are often meticulous in their habits and work and follow-up to insure completion of projects or tasks.

Each of the four areas measured falls into one of three levels of action: Prevent, Respond, or Initiate. For example, if your Fact Finder score falls into the Prevent range and you are given a detailed research task, you will find every excuse available not to accomplish the task because your natural inclination is not to do these types of activities. This does not mean that you are not capable of doing them, but rather that your natural inclination is to not do them. Conversely, someone who scores high in Fact Finder will likely do this kind of work readily because it is a natural talent for them.

Everyone has what Kolbe calls your Natural Advantage or the areas where your natural tendencies lie. Having this knowledge about yourself and your team members can allow you to assemble more effective teams, hire people with skills and natural tendencies appropriate for the job, and build stronger work groups. The Kolbe KCI is available from:

KolbeConcepts, Inc.
3421 N. 44th Street
Phoenix, Az. 85018
Phone: 602/840-9770

All of the tools and instruments described represent a small sample of what is available to businesses. Again, it is not so important which tools you select (although clearly some are better and situationally more relevant than others), but rather how you use them and over what period of time.

It cannot be overemphasized: Our penchant for the quick fix has resulted in many of the difficult situations we currently face. Changing decades-long behaviors and corporate cultures cannot be done with a wave of a wand, with any single event or any one tool. You must make a long-term commitment to yourself and your organization to change the culture, learn and teach new skills, and have the discipline and integrity to stay the course even when things are chaotic and the budget gets tight.

All of this may, on the surface, seem overwhelming and there's no doubt that it is a major undertaking, but you must ask yourself the question, "If I continue to operate in the way I have in the past, will I be able to ensure my future success?" If you can honestly answer in the affirmative, then my guess is that you have already accomplished most or all of what we have been talking about. If, on the other hand, you see the need to transform your organization, you had better get started. There is no better time than now.

When looking at organizational transformation at the macro level, what I am suggesting is a kind of formula: Corporate cultural and value setting + organizational efficiency + behavioral effectiveness = never give the competition an even break. Twenty-first century organizations will be required to reinvent themselves on the fly *as a core competency.* The most effective method of successfully accomplishing this is by understanding how and why people do what they do and by becoming masters of human behavior.

The Style Analysis, Kolbe KCI, and others are valuable additions to the managerial tool kit. They provide you with useful information about the natural "gifts" that individuals possess, as well as what they have learned to do and how they have adapted their natural style to the work environment. Where organizations and managers tend to fall short with these tools is in the area of practical application of the knowledge. I have had clients say to me, "This is interesting information and it seems valuable, but what do I do with it?" This is a fair question and must be answered if companies and individuals are to gain the return on their investment of both time and money. Remember: Knowledge obtained is interesting; knowledge applied is valuable.

To effectively apply the knowledge created by these kinds of instruments, organizations are required to create a cultural norm that allows and encourages the exploration of human behavior as normal, daily business process. We must retrain ourselves to value the process as much or indeed more than the content of the work itself. The true learning and leverage for the future is in understanding why and how we do what we do. Our traditional focus has been on what we do (the content of the work itself) rather than the methods, processes, and reasons for how and why.

We must be prepared to invest additional time in our daily work routines for examination of our process. For example, when colleagues exhibit aberrant behavior in a meeting, we must invest the time in discovering what is behind the behavior and coach them on how to interact more appropriately. This is not to say that every meeting becomes some form of group psychotherapy. Quite the contrary. What we must do is discover why we do what we do and be willing to change in order to accomplish the goals we have set for ourselves and the organization. Developing the knowledge and the skills for appropriate interventions with our colleagues, as well as the techniques for managing effective change, will provide the leverage we all seek.

The basic formula for developing these skills is practice, practice, practice. Learning and change requires concerted effort, over time. Think about the first time you hit a golf ball or the first time you played tennis. How did you do? For most of us it was a humbling experience and graphically represented our need for practice. Building management skills is no different. It requires repetition and constant change. Continuous feedback is an essential piece of the learning and change process, and must be institutionalized in the organization. Positive confrontation is a skill acquired through practice as well. There is a major difference between "getting in someone's face" and confronting them on a sensitive issue in a positive fashion. The difference is in both the approach and the technique. If we are to effectively provide each other with constructive feedback and coaching, we must develop the skills.

The development of a culture that honors this kind of feedback and coaching does not happen overnight. You must be willing to try and fail, and try again. As we all know, it's not a perfect world, and with the best of intentions we will still make mistakes. The proof of a successful organizational and cultural transformation is in how we handle the mistakes. Practice confronting others, initially around issues of low consequence and then around more sensitive issues as you gain the skills. Remember to approach each confrontation not from the position of right and wrong but rather from the position of what is in the best interest of the business. Practice suspending your assumptions in these engagements and develop solutions to problems that provide a true win/win for you, your colleagues, and the organization.

Once you have established these new ways to examine your work and to interact with each other, you and your organization will be better prepared to take the next step in the transformation process.

With feedback and positive confrontation becoming commonplace in your business, taking a hard look at how you are organized and what may need to be reengineered becomes far less threatening. In my opinion, there is no "right" way to organize a business. Each situation is different and must be evaluated for the optimal structure. Whether you choose hierarchical, cross-functional teams, matrix management, or self-managed work teams as your organizational structure is not nearly as important as how the implementation is effectuated. Be sure to choose a structure that will provide you with maximum flexibility and ability to respond to your customers. All too often companies are organized for the convenience of internal operation rather than for serving their customers efficiently.

Each organizational structure offers both advantages and disadvantages. Traditional, hierarchical structures offer the simplicity of organizational clarity and reporting relationships. Additionally, they are, in many ways, "easier" to manage than other structures. Traditional organizations are oriented to "command and control" making the decision processes obvious and levels of authority clear. Authority and power tend to be based on the position one holds rather than on individual competency and measured results. While being clear and easier to administer, these structures generally do not foster teamwork and cooperation, and have proven to make customer responsiveness difficult.

Matrix management structures have proven to be valuable in certain kinds of businesses where specific, technical resources need to be mixed and matched on a project basis. Public accounting firms, professional engineering firms, architectural firms, and certain other construction-related businesses are frequently organized in a matrix form. These structures allow for maximum utilization of certain technical resources by assigning them to several projects simultaneously. For example, a structural engineer may be reporting to three or four project managers at the same time, all of whom are working on different projects.

While these structures offer efficiency, they tend to be somewhat difficult to manage, as people frequently compete for the same internal people resources, who often feel like they must serve too many masters. Additionally, matrix organizations have an operational hierarchy in the background that frequently confuses the reporting relationships further.

Cross-functional teams are yet another approach that have proven to be useful in certain situations and are, more and more, being accepted as one of the preferred structures. In the 1980s, many high tech firms began exploring the use of cross-functional teams in their product development areas. These companies were becoming increasingly frustrated with the lack of an integrated product development and delivery system and the resultant time and expense related to these efforts. Marketing would create a loosely defined product specification (which frequently was not based on credible customer input), engineering would interpret the spec and design something that they felt would be sellable and hand over a design to production that often was too difficult or expensive to manufacture in any volume. At this point in time, upper management would intervene and mandate a redesign to "get some of the cost out of the product." This redesign process created further expense and delays in getting the product to market, often resulting in the "market window" being missed.

In an attempt to streamline the process, cross-functional teams were created, where all disciplines of the company were represented. A product development team would, for instance, be comprised of people from marketing, engineering, production engineering, quality, manufacturing, and finance with the goal of getting an appropriate product to market, on time and within budget. With all of the major disciplines represented, these teams could make appropriate business judgments within specified, broad guidelines in order to accomplish their goals. These teams would form and disband as projects were begun and completed.

I always found it interesting that this team approach was seen as something new when, for decades, we have had cross-functional teams in place in nearly all organizations. We call them top management or executive teams, but they are cross-functional by their very construct. What was being done in some organizations was merely chartering project teams using the same model, but lower in the organization. A more recent model has emerged in the form of self-directed or self-managed work teams. These teams are cross-functional in some cases while in other situations they are comprised of people from the same discipline. These team models have been applied more broadly in many organizations and, in fact, are the only model used throughout some companies. They include many of the positive aspects of all of the existing organizational models in that they have a certain structure, including team leaders, they function with defined charters, and they have specific authority, and guidelines under which to operate. They tend to differ, however, in their philosophy. Self-managed work teams tend to have an external or customer-focused bias as opposed to a more traditional internal slant. They exist primarily to move decision making closer to the customer in order to become more responsive. In general, they operate in a cooperative fashion with only the broadest of guidelines. They tend to be measured on the results they achieve, not the rules they follow, and they interface with other teams throughout the organization both formally and on an ad hoc, as required, basis.

As with all organizational models, there tends to be a structural hierarchy operating in the background. The major difference between the traditional and the team models is the function of that hierarchy. In the traditional models, management is charged with running the company; in the team based models, management serves as support to the teams.

Regardless of the structure you choose for your company, bear in mind that during any organizational transformation or reorganization process, people will be emotionally stoked, and many will have difficulty just doing their job effectively, never mind participating in the reorganization process. Be prepared to manage the fear, uncertainty, and doubt (FUD factor) that accompany any change initiative. Some people in the organization will be at risk, some may be reassigned, and others may actually lose their jobs. This is a fact of life in today's ever-changing, competitive world. Using the tools and skills you have developed to address these sensitive issues will smooth the process and provide you with a framework and context in which to deal with the human problems that emerge.

When you have chosen a structural model that meets the needs of your organization and your customers, reengineering each major function in the company is a next logical step. Reengineering is another exercise in "tap dancing through a mine field" when it comes to people and their feelings. Those that remain following the reorganization may be shell-shocked and unable to cope with what is yet to come. It is essential to provide support for groups and individuals to help them through these difficult times. Your dialog group can serve as a barometer for what's going on in the company. Be sure that people throughout the organization are talking about what is going on in a positive manner, and that they have sufficient time and opportunity to vent their frustrations and express their fears and anxiety. Any reengineering is very unsettling, and people will react to the changes in a wide variety of ways. Some will be openly hostile, others will shut down and become ineffective in their jobs, while others will consciously or unconsciously sabotage many of the initiatives and new structures.

This is a phase when it is impossible to over communicate. During periods of rapid change, I recommend you subscribe to what I call the "until further notice" management style. That is to say, keep everyone informed as to what is going on and let them know that many of the ultimate outcomes are unknown at this time but that you will communicate with them regularly as the organization discovers what it needs to do and how it is going to go about it. Reengineering, just like the initial reorganization, puts people's jobs at risk and they know it. There is nothing you can do about that except to communicate the realities of the situation regularly. Remain focused on the big picture. Be clear that the steps that are being taken are meant to insure the long-term viability of the business and that failure to take these steps puts everyone's jobs at risk, not just some.

Your reengineering efforts should be focused on creating efficient business processes that serve your customers effectively. Many reengineering efforts have resulted in increased internal efficiencies that have failed to translate into increased business and customer service. If you are going to disrupt your organization to this degree, you better create an outcome that has a positive impact on both the top and bottom lines or you have just undertaken a very expensive exercise for the sake of the exercise. Always be asking yourself and your colleagues, "How will this change allow us to better serve our customers?" If you cannot easily answer this question, you need to dig deeper into the reasons for making the change. You may, however, from time to time develop a situation where the change does not provide for increased customer service but rather offers actual, internal increased efficiencies. In these situations, an appropriate question to ask is, "How will this change impact our ability to serve our customers?" If the decision is neutral in terms of overall customer service and saves money internally, it is probably a good decision. Even if the decision causes a certain decrease in your ability to serve and respond to your customers, you may choose to make it because of the cost savings. This is a typical risk/reward decision and these are made every day throughout your organization. What is important here is not specifically whether or not this increases your ability to serve your customers, but rather if it is the correct decision for your business.

Some may argue that reengineering should precede any reorganization and that an appropriate organizational structure will emerge from the reengineering efforts. Others (like myself) will recommend choosing the structure first because the organizational structure should reflect the core values of the company. No matter how you choose to approach your transformation, remain aware that the success or failure of the outcome rests with the people and their abilities to deal effectively with both the transition and the ultimate outcome. As your organizational transformation proceeds, you will find it increasingly necessary to master new skills to manage the behaviors triggered by the changes you are making. To aid you in this pursuit, we reference a series of tools used regularly in our workshops. These tools can be used in exercise or role play situations, or on a "real time" basis in day-to-day work situations. It is critical for people throughout your organization to understand the various psychological roles and states that people operate from and how to recognize and deal with them proactively.

The first tool is an adaptation of Stephen Karpman's M.D. Drama Triangle. This is one of the most effective tools I apply in my work as a consultant. People relate to it almost immediately and understand how the various psychological states relate to one another. Karpman developed the Drama Triangle based on three psychological roles that we all play in our lives: Rescurer, Victim, and Persecutor. Each of us has operated from these various states at one time or another. Most people, however, have a scripted "favorite" position and a primary drama switch. Karpman named this tool the Drama Triangle because the drama occurs when there is a switch from one's favored position to their primary switch position.

For example, let's say a woman habitually operates from the position of Rescuer. People around her have learned, consciously or unconsciously, that she normally is the first person to help in most situations. She always seems to be trying to "fix" things or people, and routinely offers help and support even where and when it is not requested. Then, without notice, she loses her temper and begins to yell at the people around her. The "drama" has occurred in the switch from her favored, "primary" position to the favored "switch" position. In other words, she "switched" from Rescuer to Persecutor, catching her colleagues off guard. The people around her at this time are emotionally stunned by her out-of-character behavior and may unconsciously be seduced into an escalation that results in an argument without even being aware that they have been "hooked" by *her* behavior.

Another example would be a man who is seen by his wife as a big, strong, capable person, successful in business and as someone who is almost always is in charge and in control. He is normally ahead of most people and routinely criticizes others who, in his estimation, have lesser skills. However, on weekends around the house he whines endlessly about having to do the projects and chores that are a normal part of home ownership. The switch occurs when he moves from being the strong, capable man to the whiny, "Why me, why does everything happen to me? Everything I touch turns to garbage, I hate doing these projects!" He has switched from his primary position of Persecutor to Victim, thus confusing his wife with the sudden change in behavior. Many major screaming matches have been triggered by this simple switch in scripted behavior and, at the time, most people are not even aware of what has happened.

Victims, Rescuers, and Persecutors have some classic behaviors and most people are able to identify their own favored position, as well as many of the people's around them, once they are made aware of the fact that these dynamics exist in all human behavior.

I mentioned that we have adapted the Drama Triangle for use in the corporate setting and while this is true, it is actually more of an addition that an adaptation. Where Karpman has identified the negative or dysfunctional aspects of these scripted positions, we felt that offering a positive or functional alternative would help people to practice (and therefore develop) more appropriate behaviors. In our executive workshops and retreats, we use these tools to demonstrate not only that everyone exhibits these behaviors but how to recognize them and what to do about them when they surface.

The positive or functional side of Victim, Persecutor, and Rescuer, developed by Lewis Quinby, L.C.S.W., are Vulnerable, Persevere, and Reach Out, respectively. These defined behaviors provide people with alternatives to the more problematic ones described in the Drama Triangle.

As you contrast the two sides of these behaviors, some constants begin to become obvious. On the functional side, there is a certain quality to the conducts that is based upon clarity and healthy limit setting. Endless reaching out without boundaries becomes rescuing. Persevering at an inappropriate level or around dead issues can become persecuting whereas being vulnerable, again without good, healthy limits, can set you up for the victim role.

As you begin to learn and use these types of tools in your organization, be cautious, as you are dealing with people at the emotional level and you must be prepared to handle any situations that arise during application. This is not to say that these kinds of tools are dangerous or need to be used only by a trained therapist or consultant. What is important to understand is that you may get responses to some of your interventions that require skills and knowledge different from that of the traditional manager or executive. These kinds of tools need to be introduced gently, over a long period of time because, after all, their effectiveness is based not only on the skill of the person using them but on the trust shared by the people involved.

Whenever I begin a new consulting engagement, I routinely tell my clients that it would be inappropriate for them to trust me indiscriminately right off the bat. After all, other than information from a good referral source or general reputation, they don't know me from a load of hay. Sharing your deepest, darkest secrets with a total stranger is asking for trouble. Trust needs to be earned. Selective sharing, showing vulnerability situationally, and respecting confidentiality around certain issues builds trust.

Now, let's be clear that this tool (or any other single tool) cannot solve all of the behavioral issues in you organization. What you are doing is introducing the concept of human behavioral knowledge as a management technique and providing some specific aids to facilitate learning.

Our next tool is based on Eric Berne's psychological theory and practice of Transactional Analysis, or T.A. as it is popularly known. We have chosen to use T.A. for our work in the business community for a variety of reasons. First of all, T. A is mechanistic in its construct and therefore appeals to the left brain or analytical side of people. T. A., being somewhat linear in its application, has been proven to be more readily accepted. Had we chosen to use Jungian archetypal, Gestalt-oriented exercises, or Freudian-based models, I believe we would have experienced increased resistance based solely on some people's interpretation of what these areas represent.

Next, T.A. is relatively easy to understand and is intuitively correct for many people. It just makes sense when we deal with it at the practical application level. Also, I have experienced a number of consultants and clinicians working in business environments and business people themselves who already have either a passing or working knowledge of T. A., which lowers the barriers to application.

T.A. is based on the premise that every healthy human being has an internal Parent, Adult, and Child. Berne referred to these groupings of behaviors or internal belief systems as "ego states." With study and application, one can routinely identify which of these ego states one's self or others are operating from in any interaction. This knowledge is useful in choosing to exhibit certain functional behaviors that may be counter to our early life scripting. In other words, we can choose to behave differently if we know where many of our immediate, knee jerk responses come from. Since Transactional Analysis is just that, an analysis of transactions between human beings, using it, enables us to study, learn, and predict human behavior in ourselves and in others.

This tool provides you with the ability to recognize both the functional and dysfunctional behaviors defined by T.A. and, therefore, the ability to develop appropriate managerial interventions to coach your colleagues competently.

What we have described here is admittedly a cursory overview of Transactional Analysis and is intended only to provide you with an awareness of its existence and how knowledge of this type of psychological approach can be useful in a business setting. In truth, human behavior is a much more complex set of behaviors and interrelated actions and reactions than has been delineated in these few paragraphs. For an in-depth understanding of T. A. and its workings, I recommend reading *Born To Win* (Muriel James & Dorothy Jongeward, Addison-Wesley, 1971).

The last in this series of tools deals with the issues of organization, power, and thinking. The Organization, Power, and Thinking (OPT) tool is used in the transformational process when you are examining your organizational structure. We have employed the same design as in the previous two (identifying both functional and dysfunctional sides), but this tool differs in that it is concerned with corporate cultural and thinking styles rather than specific behaviors. OPT is most useful when you are transforming a traditional hierarchical structure into a team-based model.

Over the years, organizations have developed structures, thinking styles, and ways of handling power and control that match their structures. These styles tend to support the behaviors that continually reinforce the model. OPT provides you with concrete examples of the contrasts in behavioral styles that exist in both the hierarchical and team-based structures. OPT is especially helpful in identify behaviors that do not match the organizational model you have chosen.

Most organizations possess a definable culture to which people must adapt their styles and behaviors or, generally speaking, they will not "fit in." Many aspects of these various cultures are positive and productive, whereas others are intended to protect power, control, territory, and the status quo. What is important in any organizational transformation is to recognize the cultural "norms" that are helpful (that is, support the behaviors you want to reinforce) and to be able to identify those elements that need to change. In other words, don't throw the baby out with the bath water.

Some of these cultural norms are visible and obvious while others operate more in the background and are just "generally understood" by people. For example, some organizations overtly publish a dress code for various employees; others do not formalize this requirement but rather model a certain type of dress that is "expected" to be followed. While both ways result in a certain amount of compliance, the unspoken requirement is left open to interpretation by each individual. Those who choose to not follow the majority of people in the organization tend to "stick out," and are often seen as less than good company types by many of the powers that be.

A more personal example involved a high-tech manufacturing company I worked for in a managerial role earlier in my career. As one of their benefits or inducements for joining the company, they offered a four-day work week. Working four 10-hour days and having every Friday off was appealing to me, and was one of the reasons I chose that particular company. After I was onboard for a few months, several of my colleagues began mentioning to me that they had not seen me in on Fridays and were curious as to the reason. I replied simply that "we worked a four-day week and I really enjoyed having Fridays off." They then made me aware that Friday was the day when you made yourself available to meet with the president on an informal basis and that if I really wanted to get ahead in this company, I had better start showing up on Fridays. So much for the four-day work week.

In Japan, compliance is a social requirement that is rarely questioned and is generally accepted as a condition for living in that particular society. The Japanese have an expression that clearly articulates their feelings on compliance: "The nail that sticks up gets hammered down." While some of these cultural norms are changing in their society, many still remain unchallenged.

I am not suggesting that compliance is either good or bad. What we need to clarify in our organizations is which policies, procedures, and value-based cultural norms require compliance and which ones are open to interpretation and modification. OPT was designed to assist you in clarifying the behaviors that best support the team-based organizational model as you transform both your structure and your culture.

There is no doubt that this combination of compliance and freedom to challenge is often confusing to many people. Clearly, people in our society are rule followers and most are comfortable with a fair amount of structure in their lives. They would prefer things to be one way or another, black or white, right or wrong, so they don't have to occupy themselves with figuring out (thinking about) what they are doing. Much of *your* job is to become comfortable with ambiguity and to get others in your organization to achieve that same comfort level.

The dysfunctional side of OPT deals with many of the characteristics of traditional hierarchical organizations that have allowed themselves to become heavily layered and power-based. This tool, when used in actual practice, helps define the linkage between how we conduct our businesses and the behaviors that certain structures foster. In this case, when we use the term "dysfunctional," it is in terms of specific structures and behaviors in hierarchical organizations compared to structures and behaviors in flatter team-based organizations.

On the functional side of the tool, we contrast the cultural norms of a flatter, team-based learning organization with that of the traditional hierarchical structure. Again, using this tool helps define the linkage between how we are organized, our daily business practices, and the specific behaviors that these things drive.

By way of example, during a recent client meeting with a health care delivery organization, the transformation team ran into a typical hurdle when attempting to identify the decision-making guidelines for their self-managed, clinical work teams. The team had been working extremely well for about four to six weeks when they came upon their first real "sticky" issue. The work team structure had been decided and all along, the transformation team had stated how one of their goals was to have each work team function as if it were an independent, small business. This entailed new business development as well as expense management and bottom-line accountability.

A snag was hit when the subject of reimbursement from third-party payers (insurance companies, Medicare, etc.) was discussed. Certain of the team members offered that they felt some physician referrals should be refused because the reimbursing entity did not pay enough for the service. The Executive Director (the only member of top management on the transformation team) expressed his concern that refusing a physician request for service could jeopardize the relationship for future referral business and he wanted to ensure that did not happen. At this point he and the team had to deal with the reality of operating in their chosen new structure, and this realization elevated some member's anxiety. As the discussion proceeded, it became clear that while the Executive Director was very committed to the new structure, he was not yet comfortable letting go of his decision making authority when it came to taking certain business risks. At that time, we referred to the OPT tool to help the team see how the Executive Director's thinking was more aligned with the traditional, hierarchical model and that this style would not be appropriate in the team-based structure being implemented.

As we continued to examine our overall goals and the need for this type of decision making closer to the customer, he began to relax and became convinced that we were going to have to take some risks in order to accomplish the transformation. We decided that as we implemented the clinical teams, team members would receive training and analytical tools to aid them in making business decisions. Each team would participate in case study exercises and practice solving typical business problems where they were charged with the overall financial responsibility.

Without a tool of this type, the group may have polarized around this issue and not had the opportunity to recognize that the Executive Director's thinking was not wrong, it merely was not aligned with the organizational model they were implementing.

While initially uncomfortable, utilizing these and other behavioral and psychological tools in the work place can be the beginning of learning more about yourself and your colleagues and mastering the new skills required to manage well into the twenty-first century.

Clients tell me that they are surprised how close the process of using these tools in our workshops mirrors certain days at work. People exhibit all these functional and dysfunctional behaviors and more. Our job as managers and leaders is to build our skills in recognizing these behaviors in ourselves and others and taking appropriate corrective action when we observe them. These behavioral "course corrections" can do more to improve the productivity and quality of life at work than any other thing you can do. Using specific tools can accelerate your learning and, therefore, the transformation process.

There are a myriad of other styles and types of psychological tools and assessment instruments available, almost all of which have value for what they do. It is not as important to find the perfect instrument as it is to actually use the ones you find to advantage.

Many organizations have spent considerable time and money on these types of tools only to let results die through lack of follow through. As with all learning, experiencing something once is usually not enough to create the internal know-how we desire. Practice and repetition has proven to be what causes us to learn new skills. Simply taking in data and committing it to memory does not constitute learning. Creating internal know-how (the ability to perform new skills) constitutes true learning.

The realm of human behavior is no different from any other kind of learning. You have to both study and *practice* the new skills if you are to authentically learn them.

More information on the psychological tools described here, as well as others, is available from:

The Glowan Consulting Group
1520 Emory Street
San Jose, Ca. 95126
Phone: 408/293-8572
www.glowan.com

Once you have your organizational structure in place and you have reengineered your work processes to reflect maximum efficiencies, you must now, once again, concentrate on the people. By this I do not mean to suggest that you have not considered them throughout the process. Remember I have recommended dialog groups and constant communications as well as continuous 360-degree feedback as normal business process. What I am recommending at this juncture is a conscious examination of the new organization, its functions, and the skills of the people who are to fill the new positions. To function productively in the new model, you will be challenged to objectively assess the skills and abilities of each employee.

As a method to begin this assessment process, I suggest creating a skill matrix for each position in the organization and then assessing the individual skill levels of the people who will be filling these positions. Let's be clear that this portion of the overall transformation involves a major amount of analytical work, as well as making some tough personnel decisions.

However, all of the prior work will have been in vain if this important step is missed or not done well.

Look over the sample matrix below as a model for use in your organization. This is intended to give format and structure to the process, and is usually a first step in the overall assessment of positions and individuals.

As you can see, the horizontal axis shows the job title or function and the core skills required; the vertical axis lists the individuals by name. Opposite each name is a series of boxes divided by a diagonal line that corresponds to each core skill. Using a 1 to 10 scale, with 10 being perfect, rate the individual's current level of expertise relative to the corresponding skill in the space above the diagonal line. In the space below the diagonal line, in the same box, rate the individual's ability and willingness to learn the skills and improve performance on an ongoing basis.

Field Sales Manager

Name	Computer Literacy	Leadership/ Coaching	Client Relations	Sales Skills
Susan	6 / 8	7 / 9	7 / 8	7 / 8
Bill	9 / 9	6 / 6	5 / 6	7 / 7
Fred	5 / 7	3 / 2	8 / 8	8 / 9

This rating system is admittedly subjective in nature and is not intended to serve as your sole performance appraisal tool, but rather to provide you with data regarding the level and ability of individuals relative to their current or new role in the organization. Have individuals complete the form on their own prior to meeting with the manager or team leader to discuss where they have appropriate levels of skill and where they need to improve. In today's rapidly changing environment, the bottom number (ability and/or willingness to learn) is equally or perhaps even more important than an individual's current level of skill in any given area. You may find through this analysis that certain people will never be able to perform at the level required due to either aptitude or attitude. In any event, this analysis supplies you with information on where your coaching needs to go and can serve as a basis for individual development plans for all employees.

In the sample provided, notice the low score in the bottom of the rating box for Leadership/Coaching opposite Fred's name. This is an indication that he may never be able or willing to become an effective leader and therefore may be better suited for an individual contributor role in the sales organization. It is in these critical and crucial analyses that the really tough decisions must be made. This is also where most organizational transformation initiatives falter. Managers are reticent to make the tough decisions for all the reasons you probably already know. You'll hear or even say things like, "Fred has been with the company for a long time and he was instrumental to our success in the early days. I just can't let him go" or, "He's a really nice guy. Everybody likes him and if we let him go, it will have a severe impact on morale" or a variety of other excuses to not deal appropriately with Fred who may be in an inappropriate position for his skill set.

Nobody is recommending that you go through your organization with a meat axe and eliminate half the company. What I *am* suggesting is a thoughtful, objective assessment of the talent on hand compared to the mission and goals of the company. Wherever you have borderline situations, it may be more prudent to retain individuals and provide support and coaching for them to improve their skills in the area needed or transfer them to a job more properly aligned with their skills. This is frequently the best decision you can make. You retain a good, solid employee who can contribute to the continued success of the company and, together, the two of you will work to improve the necessary skills.

A word of caution here. If you know you have a major

mismatch, don't procrastinate on making the tough decision. In my experience, 80 percent of managerial time goes into marginal employees. The really bad actors are obvious and are self-selected out relatively quickly by their behavior. The stars are equally obvious and do not require a great deal of managerial review. It's the people in the middle that are the black hole for managerial time, and the really tough part is that they are usually nice people. So, what can happen to our managers is that they get involved at the personal level with employees who are chronic marginal performers. They take such employees on as their own personal cause. You will hear them say things like, "I'm going to save old Fred if it kills me" . . . . and it will.

Marginal employees are frequently people who seem to have their own personal black cloud that follows them around. They always have a reasonable excuse for their lack of performance: The car broke, the cat died, their spouse is sick, or they have just experienced their tenth physical injury of the year. While all of these things may be true, the question that managers have to continually ask themselves is, "Can I afford to have these kind of people on my team?" These people will consciously or unconsciously drain you dry. They will dominate your time and while you are pouring all of your energies into continually rescuing them, the top performers on your team resent it tremendously.

Be aware of the message you send when you do not deal with marginal performers. Your top performers see you putting so much energy into the very people that they have been carrying for months or even years. They will say things like, "I can't believe Fred is still here, he hasn't carried his own weight for years. I wonder what it takes to get fired around here?" and many other comments you have all heard or made yourself.

This is the area where your human behavioral skills will serve you most dramatically. Once you are able to observe work performance as separate from the individual performing the work, you will be on the road to greater objectivity in assessing performance. When you are able to identify people who live in the victim role, it will be easier for you to remain detached emotionally and coach well. When you are clear about your expectations, communicate regularly and coach appropriately, you never have to fire anyone, they self-select out by their own behavior. At that point, it is no longer personal, it's just business.

Now, I am not suggesting that you will ever enjoy this aspect of the managerial job. To this day, if I have to terminate an employee, I don't sleep well the night before and I'm drinking early the night after, but I am able to perform this portion of the managerial job *when it is required.*

Being clear about the goals and objectives of the company, behaving according to the published values, communicating regularly as things change, providing each other with regular, constructive feedback, and managing with integrity when it comes to performance is the essence of organizational transformation for the entire enterprise.

CHAPTER EIGHT

Making It Stick

After all the reengineering, all the quality teams, all the restructuring and transformation initiatives, how can you be expected to continue at such a pace while continuing to operate your business successfully? Realistically, I do not believe you can. By now, if you have not achieved integration of the values and cultural norms you have sought, I would expect you to run out of energy for continuing the process. However, if you have done a reasonable job of your transformation process, you will not have to continue at this "break neck" pace, the organization will do it for you. After all, your overall goal in this extended process was to transform your organization into a dynamic, flexible enterprise comprised of great people who will carry the mantle for each other, and that includes *you*.

Now is when your role begins to shift from change agent and driver to steward of the culture. As people leave and are replaced with new talent, and as your organization grows over time, new people will have to be integrated into *your* culture. This integration must be intentional. You and your team must establish policies and practices that guarantee new employees are made aware of the specific cultural norms and the personal responsibilities that allow them to live up to the values and standards required for continued employment. This will not be smooth, as we all come from different backgrounds and experiences and most of us have not operated in an open, trusting environment where personal responsibility and measurable results determine your ability to succeed and prosper.

You must completely redesign the processes by which you attract people to your organization, screen them for potential employment, and measure their ongoing contribution to the success of the company. You must attract people with a positive attitude about learning and change and the aptitude to accomplish those things. You must develop the discipline to ask tough interview questions, test for personality, philosophical, and attitudinal compatibility, as well as technical competence. People must respect working in your organization. After all, you have invested heavily in time, money, and hard work to achieve cultural transformation and you cannot afford to have individuals or groups erode the progress you have made. Be proud of your culture. Be clear with prospective and current employees about your commitment to sustaining it into the future.

I have been inside organizations where the culture is unsavory, where true arrogance exists. Organizations who believe they are doing people a favor to employ them and that people should feel "lucky" to work there are not healthy places to associate with. The new work contract is truly an alignment of the needs of both the employer and the employee in an equal partnership for the mutual benefit of both. In this environment, both are lucky to benefit from the association.

Many of the tools we have discussed can assist you and your team members in screening and integrating new members into your organization. What is crucial here is that the new culture not only supports these values but practices them by having policies and procedures that *guarantee* them. With the best of intentions, busy people will slip back into old habits and cut corners when things get tight. You must avoid these natural tendencies to backslide or all of your work will have been for nothing.

An ongoing dialog group is one vehicle for keeping your finger on the pulse of your organization, along with 360-degree feedback and organizational health surveys. Organizations, just like individuals or machines, cannot sustain themselves without periodic maintenance. Teams need maintenance just like your copy machine or they, too, will breakdown. This maintenance must become institutionalized in your organization.

You must ensure that your continuous learning culture survives and thrives. All employees must be constantly retooling their skills in order to remain competitive. Theodore Levitt of the Harvard Business School offers this observation on how to be an effective manager: "Most managers manage for yesterday's conditions, because yesterday is where they got their experiences and had their successes. But management is about tomorrow, not yesterday. Tomorrow concerns what should be done, not what has been done. 'Should' is determined by the external environment—what competitors (old, new, and potential) can and might do, the choices this will give customers, the rules constantly being changed by governments and other players, demographic changes, advances in generalized knowledge and technology, changing ecology and public sentiments, and the like." Mr. Levitt's insights offer a glimpse into the future for us all. If you are to remain competitive in your business, you must be constantly managing for the future. Managing change successfully requires knowledge, talent, and courage. If any of these elements are absent, you may not survive in the the business environment of the twenty-first century.

As your new culture begins to mature, be diligent about maintaining the integrity of your organization and its values. During times of stress caused by rapid growth or decline, uncertain market conditions or other factors, people will tend to return to the behaviors that have served them for many years. Signs of territorialism, blaming others for failures, and a general lack of individuals taking responsibility can return before you know it. Do not let these trends get a foothold! Take swift corrective action at the first signs of the old behaviors returning.

One way to ensure that your organization does not return to the behaviors of the past is to never stop your transformation effort. Continue to learn and grow and constantly challenge your colleagues to do the same. Don't be satisfied with any new status quo you seem to have achieved. Remember the status quo of the future is constant change. Continue to assist your organization in its evolution. Constantly evaluate new organizational possibilities as your business and your markets change. Always be aware of the walls people will build around themselves and their functions if allowed to. Strive to create an organization without boundaries, where the only concern is successfully serving the customer. Boundaryless organizations are identified by a distinct lack of attachment to any particular "turf." Monitor for signs of regression constantly.

People are tribal by nature and have a basic need to belong to or identify with something. In traditional organizations, this belonging has usually been provided by the functional departments they work in or by the technical speciality in which they have been educated. This belonging has provided people with a sense of identity and has placed them in certain social and economic stratas. We have identified certain people as being "professional," such as doctors, lawyers, accountants, and the like, while others are considered in different lights. While this belonging syndrome has served people at certain emotional levels, it has done more to stifle the flexibility and creativity of many organizations than anything else.

Notice the attachment many people have to professional or college sports teams. Some are fanatical about their allegiance to a particular area's team or college. They not only identify with the team and its goals of being Number One, they also actually draw some of their own identity and self-worth from this affiliation. While this, on the surface, seems benign enough, in many cases an unhealthy dynamic emerges where people are not only loyal to their particular team of choice but vilify and, in extreme cases, actually hate the other team, as if their very existence is something to be challenged. You will hear them say, "I hate such and such team, we'll kill them this weekend"—and they mean it. Of course a healthy interest in sports teams or anything else is not a bad thing. People all over the world gain great pleasure from supporting their team and enjoying the melodrama of booing the bad guys and cheering the home town heros. What I am suggesting is that when such identity begins to effect one's judgement, when people truly cannot see the individual under the uniform and actually "hate" the other players, they are in danger of losing their perspective on reality.

In the work place, for example, you will hear people in accounting say that they "hate" sales people. They accuse them of always wanting to give away the store, or sales people will resent engineers because they do not understand customers the way the sales reps think they should. These biases (or any number of others you may have heard or held) and our attachment to our particular group is where we get into trouble organizationally. Boundaryless organizations that have evolved beyond these simple attachments and biases hold a broader view of their business. In these types of organizations, people move seamlessly from functional area to functional area without any thoughts of turf or attachment. In these organizations, people are preoccupied with the mission and vision of the enterprise and generally do not concern themselves with who's "turf" is being affected by a particular decision or situation, but rather what is the best business decision to be made. In these organizations, people draw their identity from themselves and the contribution they and their colleagues make to the overall success of the business. This is where solid teamwork exists.

In some of my recent client work with an international accounting firm, we ran across a classic example of identity and turf getting in the way of executing a valid business strategy successfully. The firm had been organized and managed along traditional lines for years, and people identified with their particular technical speciality first. They were organized by those specialities—tax, audit, speciality tax, and management consulting. Rewards and recognition systems were aligned with this model, and promotions up the hierarchy followed the same model.

In an attempt to broaden their service offering to their clients, the company decided to form industry groups and assemble cross-functional industry teams to market and deliver to specific, vertical industries, such as construction, manufacturing, not for profits., etc. The teams were formed, team leaders selected, goals set, and strategies and tactics rolled out. At the same time, nothing was changed in terms of the traditional reporting relationships, titles, or rewards and recognition systems. Individual team members still reported to the Tax Partner or the Audit Partner or the Consulting Partner and while, in the context of the team, they reported to the team leader, this relationship was viewed as secondary. As you might expect, some team members (particularly the younger ones) embraced the new model with enthusiasm while the others (especially the senior members and partners) either resisted openly or did not support the new model by refusing to attend team meetings or participate in new initiatives. The results were as expected: a general lack of success in achieving the team goals and their individual portions of those goals and an overall failure of the team model.

What went wrong here was a basic lack of understanding of human behavior and people's attachment to their particular position in the firm and in the industry. Industry wide, people have always identified themselves as a tax person or an audit person or a consultant, not a team member. These belief systems will not change merely because management does something with an organization chart. People must be given incentives for making the tough changes required to learn new skills and behaviors and undergo consequences for refusing to do so. In this case, neither were provided. No "What's in it for me" and no consequences for inappropriate behavior equals no change.

As in so many of these situations what gets blamed for the lack of success is the model itself. Let's be clear, there was absolutely nothing wrong with the team model they selected. Where they failed to succeed was in the *execution* of the new model.

As new people enter your organization, they, too, will have their own set of attitudes, belief systems, and biases about how organizations should be run and where they should fit in based on their past experience. How you handle their selection and integration will determine, for the most part, how successful you are in sustaining your new culture.

Another important factor in making your organizational transformation stick is teaching your organization to continually innovate. Innovation is the cornerstone of successful businesses and one of the most difficult pieces of organizational culture to foster. Innovation involves risk, and most of us in business are risk averse, largely because we have been taught to be risk averse in life. From early childhood we are constantly bombarded with messages of what not to do: "Be careful," "Don't do that," "No, that's wrong," "You should do it this way," and so on. These negative messages translate into self-limiting beliefs that frequently result in self-limiting thoughts such as "I can't," "I won't," or "I Shouldn't."

Some years ago during a public lecture Robert Fritz, a creativity consultant, detailed a study in which children carried tape recorders to find out what kind of messages they received from their parents and teachers. When the tapes were analyzed, about 90 percent of the messages were statements of a limiting nature, such as those in the previous paragraph. Social philosopher George Ainsworth-Land has referred to a study of the potential among different age groups. At age 5, he reported, 98 percent of those tested were judged to have high potential for innovation; at age 10, the number had dropped to 32 percent; at age 15, it was down to 12 percent; and by age 30, only 2 percent were judged to have high potential to be innovative. At age 60, the number had risen to 7 percent and was climbing. People over age sixty were found to pick up new and innovative ideas faster than any other age group!

These and other studies have confirmed what we see everyday in our business lives. As we become educated in the ways of our society, we become less likely to test the boundaries and step outside the accepted ways of believing and behaving. When we reach a certain age and station in life, we become less concerned with the societal norms and what people think and are more willing to challenge the rules and behave in innovative ways. It is this willingness to challenge and innovate that we must foster in our organizations if we are to fully realize the potential of the people within them.

In Sabina Spencer and John Adams' book *Life Changes* (Impact Publishers, 1990), the authors identify ten steps for living with changes that I find relate directly to organizational transformation. They are:

1. Be patient with yourself
2. Don't be afraid to reach out
3. Look forward
4. Stay open-minded
5. Be good to yourself
6. Go for walks
7. Create small successes
8. Take some risks
9. Dream a little
10. Celebrate

Patience is an essential element of any transformation effort. Enter into the process with the long range in mind. Do not expect dramatic, short-term results because you are simply not likely to get them.

Surround yourself with good, solid support systems. Do no attempt to do this work in isolation. Reach out for help and support from within your organization and outside.

Be willing and enthusiastic about creating the future. Remember that redesigning the past will not get you where you need to go.

Always remain open to the new information you will discover during the journey. You will learn more from observing and listening than you will from telling people what to do. Be willing to have your mind changed based on better ideas, data, and intuition.

Take care to nurture yourself and counsel others in the process to do the same. Transformational work can be unsettling and maintaining balance in your overall life during the transformation process is essential if you are to have full access to your creativity and innovativeness.

Additional balance can be achieved through physical exercise of all types. When things really get tough, go for a walk to clear your mind and re-energize yourself. Frequently, ten minutes of fresh air and mild exercise can do more to help you regain your perspective than anything you can do in the moment.

Look for and create small successes in the early stages and throughout the transformation process. Each success is progress to build on. Do not minimize these. Recall the proverb about small acorns.

Be bold. Take some risks. Be willing to have a few failures and learn and prosper from them. Make the results of both your successes and your failures visible and public. Create an environment where innovation and risk taking is an honored part of the culture.

Dare to dream—in and about your business. Rediscover your capacity to "wonder" and kindle that in others. Don't apologize for being passionate about your business. Be proud of it.

Celebrate everything. Business, just as life, is not easy so don't hold back when there is cause to celebrate anything. Celebrate your failures as well as your successes. This helps remind people that there is positive learning in both and that maintaining perspective is an important part of the transformation process.

Finally, enjoy the journey. There is no more important work that you can do to guarantee the future success of your business. All of your efforts will result in creating an energized, capable organization and a culture that can sustain the business for generations of employees to come.

When it is your time to move aside for new and innovative thinking, what better legacy to leave behind than the culture you have created, the people you have helped develop, and the organization that continues to succeed.

BVG